PRAISE FOR REMEMBERING WHOLENESS

Remembering Wholeness is the ultimate spiritual self-help book. It will change your life—and your world. This book is clear, powerful, and filled with light. Carol is an inspired healer who walks her talk and whose words have an immediate transforming effect.
—Lynne Finney, Author of *Windows to the Light* and *Clear Your Past, Change Your Future*.

This is truly a handbook for thriving. My copy is highlighted, dog-eared and otherwise marked completely from beginning to end. It is all the information that should have come with life, the stuff that no one ever told us, but once we hear it makes sense. It causes a lot of Ah-ha's!
—Linda Armstrong, RET, Author of *Beyond Forgiveness*

Remembering Wholeness **has illuminated my entire soul.** This book has affected my life so personally that I am tempted to have it surgically attached! I never want to be without it. Carol has a priceless gift of harmonizing nontraditional views—as far as western culture is concerned—with tradition, to the point that I felt as if I was reading my very own thoughts, finally put into perspective. I literally had the profound feeling of remembrance as I read this book. *Remembering Wholeness* is truly a solution for thriving in today's world. By following the counsel in this book, we can all achieve our greatest potential joy—not only in the future, but also here and now. Thank you, Carol, for having the courage to boldly declare these universal truths, as we have never heard them before.
—Pam Guidel, UT

A Two-Highlighter Book! This book moved me to a whole new level of understanding personal responsibility. It definitely raised the stakes in the game of life and empowered/challenged me more than most of the other self-help books I have encountered. The book contains fifty short chapters that are succinct and easy to read. Each chapter contains gems—you don't have to plow through two hundred-plus pages to get a few good kernels. Carol's insights and experience are refreshing and timely. It is truly a handbook for thriving and is based on the premise that we are whole, not dysfunctional. Right from the start it is a cut above most of what is out there. An ocean of fresh air!

—Marilyn Freeman, Energy Healer, Master Rapid Eye Therapist

All the cells in my body are on fire when I read this book. I have devoured this book. I bought it only last weekend I am almost finished with it. I read it late into the night and could not settle down into sleep until the early morning hours. I feel like all the cells in my body are on fire when I read it. So, I've switched to early morning reading! I'm trying to pace myself to take it all in, but I can't seem to make myself slow down. I am planning to start over as soon as I've read it to the end. I have heard and studied what you talk about, but seem to be understanding it or accepting it at a deeper level. Thank you for writing this amazing book.

—A Reader from Australia

I stopped underlining when I realized **I was underlining every sentence!**

—Tecia Adamson, Artist, Sculptor

My mind is spinning thinking of all the ways this book will be useful to me, my family, and my friends. **I need this information in my home and in my life.**

— Jo Remington, Utah

Reading this book opened me up inside. It was real and immediate. I opened up to the dreams of who I wanted to become for many years. **Reading it was like being filled with light.**

—A reader from England

I am enjoying and loving this book more and more. **It is beyond anything I ever thought I'd see in any one book.** I am thoroughly, thoroughly enjoying this absolutely amazing book.

—Russell Loveland, Chiropractor, Master Teacher

Before I finished the book, I felt confident and understood that **I had the power to change my life** with the assistance of spiritual powers beyond myself.

— A reader from California

Powerful stuff! I actually felt a power coming off the pages of the book as I read. I can't imagine reading it just once. It is a book I will keep going back to.

—A reader from Georgia

Sunbeams of hope burst from Carol's being. Her message is refreshing and hope-filled. She has experienced the pain and trauma life has to give and has since created buckets full of joy that she shares with a passion to all who listen to her message.

—Jon Tuttle, the author's husband

REMEMBERING WHOLENESS

A Personal Handbook *for* Thriving *in the* 21st Century

CAROL TUTTLE

ELTON-WOLF PUBLISHING

Also by Carol Tuttle:

The Path to Wholeness

Remembering Wholeness

06 05 04 03 02   1 2 3 4 5

ISBN: 1-58619-038-5

Library of Congress Control Number: 2002100582

First edition printed in 2000

Second edition 2002

Printed in the United States

"I Have a Question" by Carlfred Broderick, August, 1986 Ensign © The Church of Jesus Christ of Latter-day Saints. Reprinted by permission.

"Parable of the Little Soul and the Sun," *Conversations with God: An Uncommon Dialog; Book 3*, ©1998 by Neale Donald Walsch. Reprinted by permission of Hampton Road Publishing.

"Some Points of My Philosophy," *You Can Heal Your Life*, ©1984 by Louise Hay. Reprinted by permission of Hay House Publishing.

Excerpt from *A Return to Love*, ©1993 by Marianne Williamson. Reprinted by permission of Harper Collins Publishers.

Excerpt from *Walking Between the Worlds*, ©1997 by Gregg Braden. Reprinted by permission of Radio Bookstore Press.

Excerpts and Adaptations from the Rapid Eye Institute *Life Skills Manual* and *Technician Manuals*. Reprinted by permission of Rapid Eye Institute, Salem, Oregon.

ELTON-WOLF PUBLISHING

2505 Second Avenue Suite 515   Seattle, Washington 98121
Tel 206.748.0345 Fax 206.748.0343
www.elton-wolf.com info@elton-wolf.com
Seattle • Los Angeles

I dedicate this book to Jonathan,
my eternal companion and best friend,
to my daughters, Jennifer and Anne,
and my sons, Christopher and Mark.
Thank you for choosing to
spend this life with me.

CHALLENGES FEED US
STRUGGLES DEPLETE US

$\mathscr{C}$ONTENTS

Acknowledgments

Introduction   1

Chapter 1   Energy What?   5

Chapter 2   We Choose Every Thought We Think and We Can Create Any Thought We Want   9

Chapter 3   Energy Follows Thought and Every Subconscious and Conscious Thought Creates Our Lives   13

Chapter 4   We Choose Our Perception and Our Perception Becomes Our Reality   17

Chapter 5   Whatever We Put Out Returns to Us Multiplied   23

Chapter 6   We Create What We Experience   29

Chapter 7   Our Most Powerful Point of Creation Is in the Present Moment   35

Chapter 8   We Have Always Been Whole   39

Chapter 9   Birth Leaves an Imprint that Starts Our Life as a Struggle   45

Chapter 10   The Power and Purpose of Negative
              Emotion   53

Chapter 11   Affirmations Work   59

Chapter 12   Physical Disease Has an Emotional
              and Mental Origin   67

Chapter 13   Why We Hold on to Disease and
              Disharmony   71

Chapter 14   Energy Healing for Depression   77

Chapter 15   Healing Can Happen Quickly   83

Chapter 16   Receive Your Healing Now   87

Chapter 17   The Earth Has a Soul and Is Changing   89

Chapter 18   We Can Change the Way We Feel Instantly 91

Chapter 19   The Universe Always Holds Us
              Accountable   99

Chapter 20   Everything We Experience Outside
              Ourselves Is Just a Mirror for Us   105

Chapter 21   Your Energy Speaks Louder than
              Your Words   109

Chapter 22   How Much Joy Can You Hold?   113

Chapter 23   We Are All One   117

Chapter 24   Everyone is Psychic   123

Chapter 25   Unconditional Love Is the Most Powerful Force in the Universe   129

Chapter 26   Angels Are among Us   133

Chapter 27   How to Petition Your Angels   141

Chapter 28   The Power of Synchronicity   149

Chapter 29   You Are a Creator   153

Chapter 30   I Am Doing Everything You Teach —Why Can't I Manifest What I Want?   159

Chapter 31   Energizing Your Beliefs to Manifest More of What You Want   163

Chapter 32   Your Child May Be a Highly Evolved Master Being   167

Chapter 33   Knowledge Has Organizing Power Inherent in It   173

Chapter 34   The Purpose of the Planet   177

Chapter 35   We Lived As Spirits Before We
                   Came to Earth   179

Chapter 36   Each of Us Has Spiritual Brothers and Sisters
                   Who Are Not in Our Biological Family   189

Chapter 37   We All Made Sacred Agreements before
                   We Came to Earth   193

Chapter 38   Saviors on Mount Zion   199

Chapter 39   Do You Believe in the Real God?   207

Chapter 40   How to Have Your Own Conversation
                   with God   213

Chapter 41   Feel Your Prayers   219

Chapter 42   All the Answers Are Inside of Us   223

Chapter 43   Everyone in Your Life Plays a Part in Your
                   Play, with a Script You Have Given Them   227

Chapter 44   Since Everyone in Your Life Plays a Part in
                   Your Play—with a Script You Have Given
                   Them—You Can Change the Scripts
                   Any Time   233

Chapter 45   How to Keep Yourself Stuck   237

Chapter 46   It's About Healing Marriages, Not Breaking
Them Up   239

Chapter 47   The Ten Lies We Think Are Love   245

Chapter 48   It's About Healing Families, Not Breaking
Them Up   253

Chapter 49   Messages Your Children Need to Hear   261

Chapter 50   Your Spirit Is Whole and Complete   269

Chapter 51   Forgiveness Is Not Optional   273

Chapter 52   There Is Enough Money for Everyone   275

Chapter 53   The Universe Is Abundant   281

Chapter 54   Serving Others Helps Us Remember
Our Wholeness   283

Chapter 55   The Power of Appreciation and Gratitude   285

Chapter 56   The Test Is Ending   287

Chapter 57   Remembering Our Future   291

Chapter 58   I Believe in Christ   293

Chapter 59   There Is a Christ in All of Us   301

Chapter 60   Charity: The Pure Love of Christ   305

Afterword   307
Appendix of Prayers   309
Appendix of Self-Help Processes   313
Appendix of Helpful Resources   335
About the Author   337
Contact Information for Carol Tuttle   338

ACKNOWLEDGEMENTS

I want to first and foremost acknowledge my Father and Mother in Heaven. Thank you for creating me. I love you both and know you are proud of me. Thank you for trusting me with so much and for believing in me.

I want to express my gratitude to my parents and my brothers. Thank your for your patience and support of me over the years.

I am grateful to all the wonderful people who promised that they would show up in my life and help me. You remembered and you did it. Thank you for inspiring, instructing and playing with me. Among them, I am grateful to:

Ranae and Joseph Johnson, thank you for Founding and Directing the Rapid Eye Institute. You are dear friends that have helped more than you know.

Joseph and Carol Bennett, Lynette Butcher, Lynell Beckstrom, Christopher Hupp, and Kathryn Dillion, thank you for your excellence in training the RET processes. You taught me well, thank you.

Betty Holland and Shirley Jones, my Reiki Master/Teachers. Thank you for teaching me, I had no idea what lay ahead.

Megan Sillito, Bill Cael, Keith and Debbie Redford, Andrew DeJesus, and Megan Smith, thank you for sharing your healing gifts and talents with me. You are some of the best Rapid Eye Technicians out there.

Bill and Patty Grissom, and Linda Lile, thank you for letting me be your student.

Craig Malecker, the best Craniosacral Therapist I know.

Reid Dunbar, an amazing spiritual man, and Russell Loveland, a gifted chiropractor, this book is here thanks to your timely encouragement and direction.

My dear friends Ashley and Lanette, I love you both and thank you for your eternal friendship.

My editor Stephanie Bird, thank you for your expertise and faithful support.

Thank you to Beth Farrell and Hazel Cox and their team at Elton-Wolf Publishing. You not only helped make this book more beautiful to match it's beautiful message, you were committed to getting it out there so everyone could be blessed by it.

I am grateful for Kelli Kirkland, my publicist at Phenix and Phenix. You believed in me and this book and knew it could bless the lives of millions. Thanks for helping make that a reality.

I would also like to acknowledge all my clients who have shown me the resiliency of the human spirit. Thank you for teaching me to believe in myself as I believed in you.

$\mathscr{I}$NTRODUCTION

꙰

"Within every human being is the natural tendency and capacity to live wholeness of life—to be fully awake and aware of the holistic qualities of life while applying all the specific laws of nature to accomplish one's goals.

"It is incomplete development of the human mind that has produced the conception of a normal person as one who makes mistakes, has problems, falls sick, and is at the mercy of circumstances. When the total potential of Natural Law is awakened in human awareness, life can be lived in fulfillment, free from mistakes, problems, and illness. Higher states of consciousness and a state of wholeness are characterized by complete alertness and spontaneous use of one's full potential; command over one's destiny, with the organizing power to accomplish any worthy goal without strain; a spontaneously nourishing, life-supporting effect on everyone and everything; and the quality of bliss and wholeness pervading one's existence."[1]

I believe this statement and feel the reality of it transpiring in my life. As a spiritual therapist, teacher, and author, I have had the opportunity of assisting thousands of individuals to create more joy in their lives. In the earlier days of my work, my intention was to help people "recover" from traumatizing childhood events. As I have awakened over the years and remembered more of my wholeness, my intentions have taken

---

[1] Maharishi Vedic University WebPages. 1996.

on a higher meaning. My intention currently is to assist people to awaken themselves to their god-self and the amazing powers of creation that lie within them. To help someone to literally, biologically, become like Christ with all the capacities and powers of God is a very awesome job.

When I began to write this book I remember thinking, *Why am I writing this book?*

Pretty much everything I have to say has already been said, or so I thought! One of my favorite authors, Louise Hay, sums it up in her "Points of my Philosophy." On page five of her book *You Can Heal Your Life,* she wrote:

We are each responsible for all of our experiences.

Every thought we think is creating our future.

The point of power is always in the present moment.

Everyone suffers from self-hatred and guilt.

The bottom line for everyone is, "I'm not good enough."

It's only a thought, and a thought can be changed.

Resentment, criticism, and guilt are the most damaging patterns.

Releasing resentment will dissolve even cancer.

When we really love ourselves, everything in our life works.

We must release the past and forgive everyone.

We must be willing to begin to learn to love ourselves.

Self-approval and self-acceptance in the now are the key to positive changes.

We create every so-called "illness" in our body.[2]

2 Louise Hay. *You Can Heal Your Life.* Santa Monica, CA: Hay House. 1984. pg. 5.

Louise Hay's book was published in the early eighties and most people still don't get what she is teaching us. I am writing this book because God asked me to. He has told me that my voice and my unique experience with myself, my students, and my clients offers another look at what has existed as universal truths from the beginning of all creation. Some of the universal truths that I have come to remember in my life, that operate constantly, whether we believe them or not, are what comprise the contents of this book.

Along with these truths you will find the stories of many of my clients. It is through the experience of assisting so many that I have come to learn the principles and laws of universal creation well. The experiences of these individuals are not unique in that they represent all of us. I am sure there will be at least one or more you will relate to.

I teach people that if they come to really understand and practically apply the formula taught by the principles in this book, their lives can only thrive. Thriving is more than having a lot of money, a physically fit body, and great relationships. Thriving is a spiritual experience. You can know who you are and why you are here. In fact, if you don't, *it's time.*

Thriving is having an ongoing rich relationship with the heavens and calling upon its powers to effect tremendous outcomes in behalf of your life and others. Thriving is where we are going in the 21st Century. To thrive only in physical, temporal ways will not sustain us. We will only be able to maintain our temporal prosperity if we know how to thrive spiritually with humility. It is our destiny to thrive on all levels and in all ways in our lives. And it is up to us to initiate this creation in our lives. It is available to everyone and it is time. Please join me.

ENERGY WHAT?

Everything at its finest level of creation is energy. We are exchanging energy and silently communicating energetically with every person we meet or come into contact with. Energy impressions are always our first impressions that influence what we think or feel about others.

I am a Spiritual Therapist who uses a healing technology called Rapid Eye Technology (RET). I help people clear negative energy. I am trained as a Master/Teacher in the healing art of Reiki. I studied Reiki to learn about the mind and body as a system of energy.

As a Certified Master Level Rapid Eye Technologist, I work in the area of energy healing or energy medicine. I practice what used to be called Alternative or Holistic Health and is now being called Complementary and Integrative Medicine. Rapid Eye Technology is based on the theory that we can initiate the rapid-eye movement we experience during our sleep in an awakened state. As a result of studying REM sleep, it was shown that during this sleep state our minds and bodies are clearing overloads of heavy, negative energy that tax and create imbalances in our system. Rapid Eye Technology has shown to have the same effect of clearing at the deeper levels of our mind and body, that can sometimes take us years to clear, if at all, if left to our own natural mechanisms.

I teach clients that RET is not the healing power. It is a technology that clears the negative energy we carry and keep recreating, that blocks and interferes with the spiritual powers of healing that are available to us. As we clear this negative energy, we allow healing powers to be *awakened* within us, and for spirit to flow healing energies into all levels of our being.

Clearing is one part of the healing process. The other part is learning new life skills that incorporate living by spiritual truths in a practical way so that we can maintain and continue to increase our state of well-being. I tell clients that they come in focused on recovery and clearing the negative, and graduate to creating and manifesting the future.

Ranae Johnson, Ph.D., is the founder of the Rapid Eye Institute in Oregon, and the author of two books, *Reclaim Your Light Through the Miracle of Rapid Eye Technology* and *Winter's Flower*. The Rapid Eye technique was actually developed out of trying to find alternate treatments for autism! *Winter's Flower* is the heartwarming story of how it all happened as Ranae tried to find help for her autistic son. In the process, she found methods to help not only him, but thousands of other children and adults all over the world.

I believe that real healing is a spiritual process. This belief kept me away from the clinical models of therapy. I was drawn to RET because of the spiritual model it incorporated. At the spiritual level, RET assists individuals in remembering their wholeness. As negative energy is released, clients are opened to their spiritual nature. This allows them to remember who they are and why they are here. RET is a comfortable process that supports them in becoming their real self— naturally and gracefully.

There are many modalities of energy healing available. Obviously, I feel RET is one of the best or I would be practicing something else! You can judge for yourself. To learn more about it, or to find a practitioner in your area, please refer to the Appendix of Helpful Resources in the back of the book.

CHAPTER 2

WE CHOOSE EVERY THOUGHT WE THINK AND WE CAN CREATE ANY THOUGHT WE WANT

We think approximately sixty thousand thoughts daily. We are always thinking. Our mind can be our best friend or our worst enemy depending on what we choose to do with it. God has given us a powerful tool that allows us to be the creators of our lives. We are completely in charge of our minds. No matter how we are feeling physically or emotionally, we are free mentally to think any thought of our choice.

Our mental body is at a higher vibration than our emotional body, meaning our minds are more powerful than our feelings. We have been trained to listen to our feelings and create thoughts that match our feelings. Therefore, if we are feeling negative feelings, we will think negative thoughts. We believe we cannot start thinking and perceiving ourselves in a positive light until we feel positive feelings. **Take charge of your life by taking charge of your thoughts. Change your life by changing your thoughts.**

Remember every time you verbalize, in private or in public, that you don't deserve this or that, you can't do this or that, or that you are less important than something or someone else, your biology will hear it and act accordingly. What do you want to tell your life force?

By thinking thoughts that make you feel good, you increase your vibration. Every person has an electromagnetic field with a vibration that sends a signal out into the world. Since we are all at quantum level patterns of light and sound frequencies, we are constantly sending messages to the Universe. The Universe is life force or matter unorganized. The Universe offers us one guarantee: that everything we put out returns to us multiplied. It is not the words you say that are most important, it is the vibration you send out to the Universe. Your thoughts are your most powerful mechanism for controlling your vibration.

Creating a strong intention in which you can hold a belief is the most powerful way to use your thoughts. Intentions are decisions, goals, ideas, wants, desires, and choices that are stated in the affirmative. A spiritual term for intention is faith. Whatever you put your *faith* in will be your life experience. When you match your intentions with a positive feeling of hope, you send a signal out to the Universe that is honored, and you receive what you have intended.

As you make decisions each day about what you want to experience, you set into motion the creation of that experience. You are the one who literally molds your future experience. As you set thoughts of what you want into motion, in combination with the excited emotion, you will be in a perfect position to receive that which you desire. The more specific you are about what you want, the more specifically you will receive that which you want. The more vague you are in stating what you want, the more vaguely you will receive that which you want.

What keeps us from asking for what we want or thinking of the ideal? Often it is our fear that we will not get it and we will be disappointed. We believe that God is in charge and it is up to him if we are to have something. We believe that what we want may not be harmonious with what God wants for us and we don't want to take the risk of asking amiss. What if God trusted us and gave us full reign to create whatever we choose for our experience? What if our ideal desire is what God wants for us, and all we have to do is make a decision, ask for it, and we then will receive it?

A common pattern of many of my clients has been to expect the worst, especially if it is something they really want. I ask them, "Why do you choose that thought?" Most explain, "Because then I am prepared when bad things happen, or I can prevent the worst from happening." I then teach them that they are setting themselves up for the worst to happen. The greatest power we have in avoiding the worst is to intend for the best to happen. I ask my clients, "If everything were going your way in this situation, what would be the ideal experience for you?" Most people cannot imagine the ideal because they have been programmed to believe that cannot happen for them.

Ask any one of my four children how much sympathy they have received from me when something is not going the way they want it to go. I am sure they would say very little. It is common to hear around our house, when someone is complaining about their life not going well, the phrases: "Why are you creating that?" or "Why are you attracting that into your life? What do you have to learn from it?" These phrases are often followed by, "What do you really want?" or, "If the ideal thing happened in this situation, what would that look like?" "You can create anything you want; what do you want to happen?"

You know you've taught your children well when you are telling your eleven-year-old to stop whining and complaining and he looks at you and says, "Why are you creating me to be this way?" The only problem with not joining your children in their pity parties is that they hold you accountable, too, and refuse to join yours.

Take the power of your mind, the power of your thoughts, and start creating the life you really want. Catch yourself thinking the worst and ask yourself in that moment, *If I could have anything I want in this situation, what would that look like?*

If your will is aligned with God's will and you really believe you deserve it, and believe it can happen, it will. If you doubt it, question it, or keep your attention on what has still not happened for you, it will kink up the energy and you will not receive it. Become the deliberate creator of your life. Anticipate your future, one second ahead or one year ahead, and be as specific and deliberate as possible and still feel good. Take time every day to identify your dominant intentions free of worrying about how they're going to show up. When you ask the powers of heaven to work in your behalf and to take care of the details, they will produce for you what you have asked for.

CHAPTER 3

ENERGY FOLLOWS THOUGHT AND EVERY SUBCONSCIOUS AND CONSCIOUS THOUGHT CREATES OUR LIVES

Everything begins as a thought. Thought joined with feeling creates emotion—energy in motion. What we believe becomes our reality. Many of our beliefs originate at the subconscious level. These sponsoring thoughts fuel our conscious, thinking mind. Our subconscious belief system is very powerful and it generates our perceptions and feelings about life. Our conscious, thinking mind is available to us at all times and can change the deeper beliefs that keep feeding into our conscious thoughts and feelings.

With a clearing tool like RET we are able to bypass the conscious mind's defense mechanisms that keep deeper beliefs and thoughts hidden away. The mind does this so we are not walking around feeling worthless and powerless all the time. By clearing deeper beliefs from the subconscious, you are then free to implement the power of positive thinking and self-affirmations more potently. All of my clients who follow this program experience improved circumstances in their lives and increased self-esteem immediately. Those who have tried using the tools of positive self-talk and affirmations to change their life but have had little or no results, realize that as they were practicing these processes, they would actually feel worse because it stirred up deeper beliefs from their subconscious minds that have been carried through the years of their lives and generations of their families.

Since this is a time of clearing negative beliefs and energies from our lives and past generations, many of us chose spirits to be the carriers of our limiting generational belief systems. If you seem to be living a life like Bill Murray, in the movie *Groundhog Day,* who kept waking up to the exact same experience day after day, and you seem to be recreating the same problems repeatedly in your life, then you are meant to clear that weakness and make it a strength. As this occurs, it is as if you break free from that weakness, and the members of your entire family line are recipients of your change. Many people in the past, present, and future, who are biologically connected to you, are released to greater possibilities.

It is like the four-minute mile. There was an energy block on a human running a mile in less than four minutes, until one person, Roger Bannister, broke through it. This allowed others to obtain the same results with less effort. There is divine purpose in your selected weaknesses. Your spirit knows the potential you have to create a contrast. Whatever challenges you are currently facing, know that literally in your biology, in your DNA, there is a blueprint of the solution with all the thoughts and feelings that will guide you to success. Know that at whatever level you have come to know pain, you can know the contrast of joy at that level. If you have known great pain and spiritual turmoil, you can know great joy and spiritual happiness.

Clearing the subconscious mind of all its limiting beliefs and emotional blocks from your prebirth, prenatal, birth, infancy, childhood, teen years, and generations before you, and choosing conscious thoughts that are honoring and loving, will allow you to realign with your soul and have continually increasing awareness of your inner spiritual wisdom.

WE CHOOSE OUR PERCEPTION AND OUR PERCEPTION BECOMES OUR REALITY

The story is told of a philosopher who stood at the gate of an ancient city greeting travelers as they entered. One of them questioned him:

"What kind of people live in your city?"

The philosopher met the question with a counterquestion: "What kind of people lived in the city from whence you came?"

"Oh, they were very bad people," answered the traveler, "cruel, deceitful, and devil-worshiping."

"That's the kind of people who live in this city," declared the philosopher.

Another traveler came by and asked the same question, to which the philosopher replied: "What kind of people lived in the city from whence you came?"

"Oh they were very good people," answered the second traveler, "kind, and truthful, and God-loving."

The philosopher replied, "That's the kind of people who live in this city."

Each of us has our own unique perception of the world, which is based on our experiences. We each have our own set of glasses to view and interpret the world around us. A difference in perception has been the cause of many an argument and has been the basis for all wars.

Your unique perception has been acquired through generational influences and through life experiences. You came into the world with tendencies towards certain beliefs and behaviors, which were influenced by your genetic inheritance. These beliefs and behaviors develop into your perceptions.

One of the greatest powers in healing that we have is the ability to change our perception, to take something that seems overwhelming and hurtful and make it seem like no big deal, or to be able to say, "it just is." We usually only have to make something a big deal if we want to be right more than we want to be happy. At any given moment you can choose to take something that seems important and make it not important to you. In that moment you release the need to be right or the need to have it go your way.

Every human being carries unmet emotional needs from their childhood into their adult life. The recovery literature of the eighties was dominated by the subjects of healing your inner-child and releasing co-dependency. The literature suggests that your inner-child is wounded and needs healing, and that your co-dependency is a dysfunctional pattern of getting those unmet needs met. What if you were to start believing today that all your childhood needs are met, and that your childhood was ideal and wonderful? Wouldn't the patterns of co-dependency eventually disappear because you had changed your perception of your childhood? Your mind does not care what memory you choose to carry: it's all your perception of the past anyway.

I used to believe it was important to know what happened to us in our childhood so we could really heal. Why? That idea just perpetuates the belief that you are a victim, which feeds the perception of life being hard. We are literally creating our own world around us with our thoughts, beliefs, and perceptions. Fear will cause us to see the world as threatening and hostile, with anger and attack as its expressions. Joy within will cause us to see the world as safe, beautiful, and helpful to us, with excitement, wonder, and gratitude as its expression.

Desire is the first and most important ingredient to healing. Clients who really want to heal and are not just looking for relief come into their sessions eager to let the past go. Clients who are still anxious to know if what they are remembering is true have a harder time. In the case of a client healing from childhood sexual abuse, one of the most common perceptions that keeps them stuck is believing that if they heal from this trauma it will be as if it never were, and no one will be held accountable for hurting them. It's almost like they have to stay in the energy of a victim until they return to God so there is evidence of wrongdoing and justice will be served. I encourage clients to change their perceptions about those who have hurt them. The following is a parable excerpted from *Conversations with god: An Uncommon Dialogue; Book 3*, that helps us understand how we can truly love those we have perceived as our enemies:

[God talking:] *"You may choose to be any part of God you wish to be,"* I said to the Little Soul. *"You are Absolute Divinity, experiencing Itself. What Aspect of Divinity do you now wish to experience as You?"*

"You mean I have a choice?" asked the Little Soul. And I answered, "Yes. You may choose to experience any Aspect of Divinity in, as, and through you."

"Okay," said the Little Soul, "then I choose Forgiveness. I want to experience my Self as that Aspect of God called Complete Forgiveness."

Well, this created a little challenge, as you can imagine.

*There was **no one to forgive**. All I have created is Perfection and Love.*

"No one to forgive?" asked the Little Soul, somewhat incredulously.

"No one," I repeated. "Look around you. Do you see any souls less perfect, less wonderful than you?"

*At this the Little Soul twirled around, and was surprised to see himself surrounded by all the souls in heaven. They had come from far and wide throughout the Kingdom, because they heard that the Little Soul was having an extraordinary **conversation with God**.*

"I see none less perfect than I!" the Little Soul exclaimed. "Who, then, shall I have to forgive?"

Just then, another soul stepped forward from the crowd. "You may forgive me," said this Friendly Soul.

"For what?" the Little Soul asked.

"I will come into your physical lifetime and do something for you to forgive," replied the Friendly Soul.

"But what? What could you, a being of such Perfect Light, do to make me want to forgive you?" the Little Soul wanted to know.

"Oh," smiled the Friendly Soul, "I'm sure we can think

of something."

"*But why would you want to do this?*" *The Little Soul could not figure out why a being of such perfection would want to slow down its vibration so much that it could actually do something "bad."*

"*Simple,*" *the Friendly Soul explained, "I would do it because I love you. You want to experience your Self as Forgiving, don't you? . . .*

"*I ask only one thing in return,*" *the Friendly Soul declared.*

"*Anything! Anything,*" *the Little Soul cried. He was excited now to know that he could experience every Divine Aspect of God. He understood, now, The Plan.*

"*In the moment that I strike you and smite you,*" *said the Friendly Soul, "in the moment that I do the worst to you that you could ever imagine—in that self-same moment . . . remember Who I Really Am.*"

"*Oh, I won't forget!*" *promised the Little Soul. "I will see you in the perfection with which I hold you now, and I will remember Who You Are, always.*"[3]

<hr />

"Love your enemies, bless them that curse you, do good to them that hate you, and pray for them which despitefully use you, and persecute you"[4]**...because they may have been your best friend in heaven.**

I know that God will give liberally to those who ask. Prayer will help us draw more fully on the powers of heaven and the powers of Christ's atonement.

[3] Neale Donald Walsch: *Conversations with god: An Uncommon Dialogue; Book 3.* Charlottesville, VA: Hampton Roads Publishing. 1998. pp. 347-49.
[4] Matthew 5:44

Therefore, lift up your voice and ask God to remove any perceptions that are stumbling blocks to you forgiving and feeling whole. Many, many times I have asked God to change my perceptions to ones that support me in feeling peace and harmony and showing up in unconditional love and allowing. I know he has assisted and will continue to assist you and me each time we ask.

CHAPTER 5

WHATEVER WE PUT OUT RETURNS TO US MULTIPLIED

We live in a universe with constant laws and truths by which even God functions. He is the master and knows how to use the laws and truths to create an unending stream of joy and happiness for his existence. "His work and his glory are to bring to pass the immortality and eternal life of man."[5] He created us so we could become like him and, like him, experience a constant stream of joy and happiness. We are here on a planet of free choice to come to a knowledge of these laws and truths and of how to become like him through experience. Through the experience of contrast, or good and evil, light and dark, we come to know who we are and what we want so we can become partners with God in creating it.

One of the basic laws of the universe is the Law of Attraction. It is the law of the harvest: we reap what we sow. The Law of Attraction is as real as the Law of Gravity. Before the Law of Gravity was identified, nobody knew it existed, and yet everyone was still affected by it. Such is the case with the Law of Attraction; most people are unaware of the mechanics of how it works and yet everyone is still affected by it. You don't need to know the mechanics of how the Law of Gravity works to keep yourself from floating off into space. You also do not need to know the mechanics of how the Law of Attraction works for it to function in your life. You will want to know so you can create a life of more well-being and harmony. You can actually be in deliberate control of your life experience, knowing what you want and manifesting it in abundance in your life. Or, you can continue to believe that life is a series of random events that you must learn to overcome, put up with, ignore, protect yourself from, or on occasion, enjoy a reprieve and experience some joy and happiness.

The Law of Attraction, simply put, is that whatever we put our attention on, in belief, thought, and feeling, will come into our life multiplied. There is no exclusion in the Law of Attraction. If you think about what you don't want, then you will get a lot of that. If you have a need to worry or complain, then you will attract a lot of people and experiences to worry and complain about. If you carry a lot of fear, you will attract life events that support that fear.

If you want to know what your deeper beliefs are, look at your life and it will tell you. Life is a mirror reflecting back at us what we believe about ourselves. If we don't learn the lesson, the experience will repeat itself and become more and more intense until we pay attention, get the information, and change our beliefs. Rapid Eye Technology helps people go to the deeper mind where the core issues and beliefs exist within us so we can easily release this energy and create a new belief, which creates a new life.

The principle that we always receive what we believe is relentless. It is in constant operation whether we notice it or not.

Many people have trouble with the belief that in order to have the good in our lives, we have to be willing to accept the bad. This creates a continual block to progressing in any real way with the quality of our lives. The universe simply gives us whatever we believe. Change your belief and you'll change your life.

What about the real-life tragedies of children who are abused, people who get into car accidents, or have life-threatening illnesses? What about people who die as innocent victims at the hands of others who choose to kill? As I write this, the tragedy of September 11, 2001, has recently occurred. Three different planes made the World Trade Center Towers and the Pentagon their targets. Both World Trade Center Towers collapsed to the ground and a large section of the Pentagon was destroyed. As a result over five thousand people lost their lives and many families were left to grieve their loved ones' passing.

Another unbelievable tragedy occurred a couple of years ago at Columbine High School in Littleton, Colorado. Two teenage boys, heavily armed and in a state of revenge, entered their high school and went on a rampage, killing several and wounding many others, finally ending the blood-bath with their own suicide. If you take what I am presenting here with no exceptions in life, this means all of these people created this carnage. Why? Believe me, I have asked this question and looked at it several different ways in the last twenty-four hours. I am on a quest to make sense and find a divine purpose in even the ugliest of humanity's actions. I believe strongly that Christ is intricately involved in this planet, and every event here is a preparation for a grander outcome.

In the cases of the events of September 11 and Columbine High School, here are some of my understandings. I do believe we have a world of free choice. We are each independent of one another in what we can experience. We each have our own independent consciousness. We also have collective consciousness. Groups of people form a collective consciousness which are collective beliefs. In the United States many people, even children, put their attention on violence and death. It is easy to find. It's all over the news; it's in our cartoons; it fills our movies; it is rampant in our video games, and we keep watching. According to the Law of Attraction, whatever we put our attention on in belief, thought and feeling will come back to us multiplied. If we keep putting our attention on violence and death, we will keep creating it in our society. Until we are entertained by peaceful means, we will have to keep continuing the experiences that become more and more tragic until we learn the lesson and change our experience by changing what we focus on.

What about the innocent victims? Why would they create this in their lives? God knew we would create adverse conditions, so he has a system of grace built into our life experience. I believe each of these souls volunteered to move on, to end their physical experience. The workings of the spirit are intricate and intimate. I believe everyone that is abused, raped, murdered, or has suffered in some other fashion was given a choice at the spirit level, and they chose suffering, and great will be their growth and reward.

Each of us chooses life adversities to perpetuate our growth and potential for more levels of light. Many innocent people have died, been hurt or abused on this planet, even Jesus Christ. I know we are all watched over and always given solutions. For every struggle, a solution already exists. I believe these very powerful, painful events occur for us to examine our lives. As a nation, all we have to do is look at what is happening in our society to know what we are believing as a collective consciousness. The solution is to put our attention on what we want rather than looking at what is happening and how we need to protect ourselves from it.

As a parent, I can believe that the world is not a safe place for my children and pass this fear onto them. If I do this, I make their chances of being victimized even greater because they will attract those people interested in hurting others. I can empower them by making them aware of contrast, that good and evil exist in this mortal dimension, and teaching them the Law of Attraction— which is that they can choose whatever they want to experience. If they want to be safe and feel good, then all they have to do is believe and they will attract only that into their lives. We do our children a great service by creating a space for them to know who they are, to love and honor them, to treat them with respect, to teach them correct principles, and to let them govern themselves, and learn from the contrast of life.

A Course in Miracles[6] teaches us this, "I am responsible for what I see (perception); I choose the feelings I experience, and I decide upon the goal I would achieve. Everything that seems to happen to me I ask for and receive as I have asked."

---

[6] *A Course in Miracles.* Glen Allen, CA: The Foundation for Inner Peace. 1975.

Our spirit provides the power to know what is wanted for us. Our mental capacity takes that energy and directs it. Our emotional body supports it with feeling good, and what is wanted flows abundantly into our lives.

WE CREATE WHAT WE EXPERIENCE

I remember when I really woke up to this truth. It made me furious, and at the same moment I experienced one of the most freeing energies I had ever felt. I was on my knees pleading with God to help me get on with my life. I still felt stuck and needed more strength to overcome the constant struggles in my life. God, or Heavenly Father as I affectionately refer to the God I believe in, told me in that moment that the reason I kept having struggles was because I kept believing I was a victim in life. I was told that I was creating it, and if I changed my belief and really believed at a cellular level that I was no longer a victim, my life would change completely.

I was angered by this feedback because if this were the case, I could no longer blame anyone else for the dysfunction in my life. I liked believing I was a victim who had learned to be a survivor, and that others and circumstances beyond my control were at fault for my struggles. I really knew how to put the blame on God and Satan as well. Weren't most of life's challenges either God trying and proving us or Satan tempting us? If I were the creator—and I mean the one that at some level influenced everything that had ever and would ever happen to me—then I was creating some pretty messed up scenarios.

I would have to own it all and I didn't like that. I still thought someone had to be blamed and now it would be me. I became very determined to really understand this truth. I knew in the moment of my anger that if this were true, then I could create something really wonderful for myself. I figured, wow, I've got real potential here. Look how good I created the things I *don't* want. If I can even be half as good at creating what I *do* want, my life could be very sweet.

Through my personal experience and my years of professionally assisting others get well, I have concluded that the deeper beliefs held in our subconscious mind can often play out to be some of the most powerful influences in what we end up creating and re-creating in our lives.

Many of our negative beliefs held about our world and ourselves were genetically passed on to us from our ancestors and established in our childhood. At that time we also started creating dysfunctional patterns to counter the negative beliefs in order to give us a sense of safety and importance in our world. As adults we can identify and clear the deeply rooted limited beliefs and dysfunctional patterns that are a byproduct of them.

Even though you may not be consciously thinking these negative beliefs about yourself, you are still sending out a powerful signal that attracts the people and events into your life that honor what still exists for you at the subconscious level.

That is why life is such a great mirror for us. If you want to know what your most powerful beliefs are about yourself—whether you are aware of them or not—just look at your life. Once I finally understood this principle I began to notice the negative aspects of my life and look at them differently.

Even after devoting many, many years to my own healing and spiritual growth, I know I am still evolving and remembering my truth. When a situation occurs that is dishonoring to me I now say to myself, *Why did I attract that? What part of me is still believing I am not lovable? I am gracefully and comfortably clearing all limited beliefs about myself on all levels. I am knowing my divine worth and everything I create is a reflection of that.*

A client may come to me unaware of some of their most powerful negative beliefs, yet their life experience is clearly shouting to them they have them. For some, those negative beliefs may be hard to accept because they spent years blocking them out from their conscious thinking mind in order to survive.

At Gary's first session I asked him how he felt about himelf, his self-confidence and self-worth. He shared that he felt fine and that he had enough self-worth and confidence. He was completely ignorant of his deeper held beliefs that kept manifesting his negative experience very obviously in his day-to-day life. That his deeply held negative beliefs were sending out powerful signals that attracted disease, disharmony, and painful events into his life. Gary came to me after coming through an experience with cancer that almost ended his physical life. He had overcome the cancer yet he was physically exhausted, depleted, and still required a lot of medication daily. He was in tremendous conflict with his wife and close to separating from her, believing she was not sensitive to his needs and "the love had gone out of their marriage." He had also been fired recently from a high-powered position because of some misconduct on his part, and at our first session he was unwilling to discuss the details of his actions. He was extremely depressed and felt hopeless. He believed that all of this life experience had "happened to him."

~

A person who knows and embraces their wholeness on all levels, and has life-skills that complement that knowing, has the evidence of a life experience that reflects this state of being.

The clients who come to see me who are aware of how their painful childhood experiences are interrupting their ability to have a healthy, joyful adult life are challenged differently.

For them the challenge often is to take ownership of what they keep recreating and stop blaming their parents or perpetrators and everything outside of them as the problem. They have acquired the perception, *These negative beliefs about myself must be true because look at what keeps happening in my life*. They are still believing their experiences create their beliefs. Very quickly I introduce them to the Universal truth: **Your beliefs create your experience.**

By identifying and clearing the negative beliefs held in your subconscious mind, by what I refer to as your "wounded inner-child," you will identify and clear the negative patterns and experiences you keep recreating.

Creating new beliefs held by your wounded inner-child subconsciously, and your adult-self consciously, makes it easy to establish new healthy patterns in your current experience. In these new thoughts and patterns you are sending out a vibration or signal that attracts back into your life more of what you want. You stop creating what you don't want and get very good at creating what you do want, which will make your life very sweet.

CHAPTER 7

OUR MOST POWERFUL POINT OF CREATION IS IN THE PRESENT MOMENT

If you don't like the life you are experiencing, **change your thoughts now.** Your future will be determined by whatever thoughts and feelings you are currently having. If you continue to believe that you can never get it right, that you are no good, that you have to keep healing and clearing and recovering, then you will. Start believing in the life that you want as if it were already happening.

At any given time you are emitting to the world a vibration that is being received by the Universe. It is your free agency to think any thought and feel any feeling that you choose. This agency is the most powerful tool that you have to change your life right now.

You are like a radio signal telling the world and the Universe who you believe you are and what you perceive your life to be. That signal goes out and that is what shows up in return to always make you right.

There is no exclusion in the Law of Attraction. If you think and worry about what you do not want, believing that is the way to fix it or safeguard yourself, you are fooling yourself. The best way to get what you don't want is to think about it a lot, talk about it a lot, and feel worried. It will show up and keep showing up. The best way to give yourself what you do want is to imagine it, get excited about it, allow it to happen, and express gratitude to God when it does.

We too often blame God or Satan for our challenging circumstances. When life is difficult we say that it is our test: it is God proving us. Or we say it is Satan tempting us or trying to control us.

What if our difficulties are a direct result of our belief that life is hard and has to be a struggle because that is how we grow and learn? That belief is one of the deepest and most widely held beliefs on this planet. It has been imprinted into the cells of every human since the creation of humanity. It has been a necessary belief structure for the purpose of this planet and the evolution of God's children into more light and truth. I believe it is the old formula for growth and spiritual enlightenment. I believe we are coming into a new age, a new energy wherein we are free to create whatever we want. If we can hold the beliefs—*I am now learning in joy and humility. God manifests his grace upon me to live in prosperity, love, and wellness, and I am serving God with my spiritual purpose in gratitude,*— then this is what we will create.

I used to believe that my adversities in life were being dealt out by God. That was how I proved myself to him. That was contradictory to my knowledge that God was all loving and all knowing. Why would he have to try me and test me if he knew me, loved me, and essentially knew the outcome of my life? I now believe that I created my own struggles, with God's support, so I could come to know myself and master my spirit by coming through the energy of pain, darkness, and spiritual hardship. Maybe to my spiritual higher self, none of this felt bad. Maybe moving through this energy in the physical world and coming out of it was like taking a ride on Space Mountain at Disneyland: It was dark and bumpy; it jerked me around; I felt out of control most of the time, and I wasn't sure when it was going to end. When I am on the Space Mountain ride, I love it. I am yelling and waving my hands in the air. Maybe if in our deepest darkest moments we could really grasp that our higher self is loving what we are going through, that it is like a wild ride, we would yell and wave our hands in the air. Our higher self really knows all is well and that the ride will come to an end.

Trust this and start right now imagining your life exactly as you want it to be. The challenge of the time in which we live is no longer how much pain can we endure, but how big can we dream, how much joy can we hold, and how long will we let it be that way? Pain and struggle are familiar to all of us, yet it is not our natural state. Our natural state is to feel good and to know happiness. I used to walk around the house repeating between fifty to one hundred times a day, "I am happy, life is easy, and it is familiar." I would notice and catch myself making life harder than it had to be and say to myself, *Some part of me is still believing I am a victim and that life has to be hard.* Then I would ask myself, *What do I want?* I want to feel good, I want to be happy, and I want others to feel good just being around me. Then I would translate that into self-affirmations and say to myself, *I am feeling good. I am happy. I am experiencing others feeling good just from being in my presence.*

Whatever you are currently dealing with, know that it no longer has to be hard or take a long time to change. Your intention to feel good right now will be honored, and your life will start to change. Keep coming back to that and think good thoughts as many times as you need to. It will become your reality.

CHAPTER 8

WE HAVE ALWAYS BEEN WHOLE

One Sunday in church the speaker suggested that we are not perfect, nor could we attain remembering our perfection in this lifetime. But, if we worked hard enough, we could get a pretty good start at it. Her message implied that it was our doings that brought us to this not-yet-perfect-but-still-trying status. I had to chuckle inside because I once believed this too. She told a story of a woman who had too much to do in her life and finally had a spiritual collapse. She couldn't keep doing all the things she was required to do to get closer to perfection. The speaker used the analogy that all of this woman's doings and responsibilities were like bricks on her back with a weight so great they almost crushed her. The speaker never said who put the bricks on the woman's back. She finished her sermon by telling us that as women, we just have to be more patient in our attainment of perfection. I thought to myself "Take the bricks off. You don't have to carry them any longer, and you never did. In fact, you are the one who put the bricks there, and, oh yeah, you are already perfect, you just forgot that you were."

God didn't put the bricks on her back; she did. She believed in *doing* perfect and forgot that the counsel is to *be* perfect. Christ already told us that he's taken our burdens so they will be light. I don't know where in any of God's teachings that he has told us that we could not become whole in this lifetime. Christ has told us that "when he shall appear, we shall be like him, for we shall see him as he is; that we may be purified even as he is pure."[7]

What is the point then? Is this earth experience just a big To Do List? I believe that we can come to a remembrance of our god-self, our I-am-perfect-just-as-God-created-me self, in this lifetime. I believe I am getting to know that part of me now. You are loved. You are already whole. You have just forgotten your wholeness. And in that forgetting you stumble and fall and make mistakes that you are meant to learn from.

We come into this world with the soul intent on remembering who we are—our gifts, our glory, our power, and our god-self. We choose an interesting way of remembering: we are remembering by experiencing who we are not. We are not powerless. We are not inferior. We are not inadequate. We are not all the thoughts and feelings that make us feel uncomfortable, disappointed, discouraged, worthless, and incapable. I have said to many of my clients that if the negative beliefs they had about themselves were true, they wouldn't be feeling negative emotions about them. They would feel satisfied. They would feel totally okay because they had tapped into their true identity. The reason they are feeling negative emotions is because they are believing what they are not, and it is very uncomfortable to exist in a lie. The negative emotion is meant to be a warning bell ringing within us and sending the message: "Warning! Warning! What you are currently believing and thinking is a lie! Continue to believe it and to think it, and you will feel worse and worse."

7 Moroni 7:48.

In the moment of noticing the negative emotion, change what you are thinking from negative to positive. Change the channel. If you are thinking, *I can never do anything right,* change it to *I am always doing the best I know how.*

Instead of Thinking:	Think:
I am worthless.	I am powerful, and I am using my power to make a difference in the world.
Other people use me.	I am attracting people who are thoughtful and considerate of me.
No one appreciates me.	I am thoughtful and considerate of myself and others.
	I appreciate myself and others appreciate me.
I can never do anything right.	I will do everything I choose to do well enough.
Life is hard.	I am experiencing my life as simple and easy.
I am having a bad day.	I am having a good day.
If something bad is going to happen it is probably going to happen to me.	Things always work out for me. My life is great.

I recommend Louise Hay's book *You Can Heal Your Life*,[8] as an excellent resource to learn the language of positive affirmations. I used this book daily to make a weakness of mine into a strength. My familiar state of mind was to think negatively. I looked at my family pedigree and recognized that a lot of my ancestors had been less than positive people and there was a fair amount of depression in my family lines. My genetic inheritance made it easier to wake up each day and think the worst, so I would be prepared for the worst. I didn't just have a chip on my shoulder, I had a substantial rock. I despised people who were naturally optimistic and positive. I perceived them as Pollyannas, who were not willing to deal with reality, because if they were dealing with reality rather than always looking on the bright side, they wouldn't be so happy.

I now know that we each have our own reality and it is created by whatever we have our attention on and by our individual perceptions. I made a conscious, verbal choice that I would become a positive thinker, and that I would create that to be my natural state. I believe through our own personal intentions and efforts and the aid of God's grace, we can make any weakness a strength. I was led to Louise Hay's book as my bible of positive talk. I learned the language, and I am very good at it now. I can honestly say it is my natural state.

As I continued my pursuit of changing my life from patterns of struggle, I noticed that my familiar state was to feel anywhere from lousy to really awful. I believed that hardship and struggle had to be a part of my life. I noticed more and more how I kept creating situations that honored these familiar feelings. It was scary to feel good. I had to get myself back into

[8] Louise Hay. *You Can Heal Your Life*. Santa Monica, CA: Hay House. 1984.

a struggle so I could feel safe and in familiar territory. I am convinced that most humans are so addicted to struggle and human drama that we daily sabotage spirit's efforts to help us make our lives simple. When our belief systems accept that with spirit all things are easy and simple, our lives and all we do will become easy and simple. We will look back and see how hard we have made our life's journeys and our relationships. It is time to simplify our lives and to move into the energy that life can be an experience of learning through joy instead of pain, and that we can live in prosperity and wellness and still serve God in humility and be Christ-like.

CHAPTER 9

BIRTH LEAVES AN IMPRINT
THAT STARTS OUR LIFE AS A STRUGGLE

There is an old energy and a new energy. The old energy patterns involve struggle, pain, blame, resentment, and anger. The new energy patterns involve love, grace, abundance and prosperity for everyone, learning through joy and ease, humility, charity, gratitude, and appreciation. The new energy honors our god-self, and we can choose to be co-creators with God. All the resources of heaven are at our disposal to make our lives grand and wonderful and attracting all that is sweet unto us.

If you are an adult, you were most likely born into the old energy pattern. Birth itself leaves an imprint of pain and struggle. Think about it. The birth process sets us up to believe that life is hard and you have to struggle to survive. You come from a spirit existence of light and love as a being of light and love. You must slow down your vibration to acquire a body. You take on all your mother's and father's emotional DNA. You grow and change rapidly to eventually have no freedom of motion because the size of the space you are in is very small and tight.

You go from that small space to an even smaller space—the birth canal—and through a tremendous amount of pain and effort, you are pushed and pulled through the birth canal. If your mother was completely anesthetized during delivery, you feel completely abandoned and feel you have to do everything on your own. How do I know this? It was one of my core beliefs as a result of my birth. I even went around complaining to my family, "Nobody is there for me. I always have to do everything by myself. I get no support!"

From the birth canal you land in an alien world with bright lights where the temperature has dropped thirty degrees. You are prodded, poked, cut, with no ability to move or speak. Most people reading this book did not have their fathers present at their birth, and they were taken away from their mothers. That's a normal birth! Throw in a few details like being born premature, a cesarean birth, drugs, induced labor, wrong sex, late birth, attempted abortion, possible miscarriage. Or add the big ones like conceived in rape or being born illegitimate, and you've got some heavy-duty energy patterns influencing your life. You have just come into the world with an overlay of energy that sets you up to believe life is hard, you have to struggle to survive, there's no support for you, there's not enough love to go around, and you do not want to be here.

In the first session, I take every client through a birth clearing. Most people are walking around with thoughts and behavior patterns that are directly related to their birth experience. You could be fighting time and have the pattern of being late to everything because you were overdue. If you were premature, you probably have beliefs and experiences such as: waiting for others, wanting everything in a hurry, feeling nervous, rushed, and running. Some other examples of birth energy residue include:

- ❖ Feeling unplanned, unwanted
- ❖ Suffering to get love
- ❖ Having to work harder than others to have anything I want
- ❖ Having to prove myself, show others I am deserving of good things
- ❖ Always checking with others for approval

If your mom was seriously ill during pregnancy or almost died at your birth, you may believe you cause others pain. You may think of others before you think of what you want. You may be afraid of your own power because you believe you can really hurt other people.

The transition from the womb to the birth canal will leave energy imprints of stuck, struggle, can't move forward, can't move back. No way out. Afraid of the future. These old energies still vibrate in us and set us up to create life experiences that honor these beliefs. Many clients say things like "I feel stuck in my life," and "I feel there's no way out!"

A cesarean section may leave patterns of sudden change, headstrong, stubborn, doing the opposite. I better get help with this or I'll never get out. Angry at being interrupted. Can't do it myself. Not going for what I want.

A forceps delivery may create a feeling of needing to be bailed out at the last minute. It's difficult to finish. Control issues. People force me. People pull me. I want to do it myself. Support leads to manipulation.

John came to me feeling tremendous guilt and
sadness over his elderly mother's death. He had lived
most of his life trying to please his mother, to no
avail. Most of the decisions of his life had been made
with her welfare in mind and how she would feel
about it. Her feelings had always been more important
than his own, and if something upset her, he would
not go through with it. John was in his mid-to-late
fifties. He had never married. He was too busy taking
care of his mother emotionally to be able to share
himself with anyone else—even himself.

I asked him at his first session about his birth experience. He said that what he knew about it was that he
was very overdue and it was a very hard and long labor
that had almost killed his mother due to complications. He
had been reminded by aunts his entire life that he should
be grateful for his mother because she almost lost her life
having him. He grew up being told, "You could have
killed your mother."

I asked him the details of his life just prior to his
mother's death. He shared that all his life he had felt
trapped and insecure, unable to make decisions for what
he wanted, always thinking of his mother. Prior to his
mother's death he had been involved in some self-help
programs learning about personal empowerment and
how to move on with your life. Through the help and
support of others he made a decision to take a new job

and relocate regardless of his mother's approval and support. His core belief was "I can't have a life of my own, because if I do it will kill my mother." Since the Universe and others honor our strongest beliefs, we will cause the things we fear the most to transpire in our lives just so we will notice them, clear them, and create a new belief. In John's case, soon after he made these big decisions, his mother became severely ill and died. By the time he found me, he had lost his new job, had moved back to his hometown, and was punishing himself for his mother's death—for which he felt responsible. He had never considered that his birth experience had influenced the choices he had made for the rest of his life.

After clearing this old energy, he was free to form new beliefs and patterns that reflected his new-found wholeness. Beliefs like:

- ❖ I am loved and supported by others.
- ❖ I have every choice available to me.
- ❖ The choices I make are appropriate, and
  I am supported.
- ❖ I am free to move on with my life.
- ❖ Life is good to me.
- ❖ My mother's higher self loves and approves of me.
- ❖ I am free of all self-imposed limitations.
- ❖ I know who I am and what I want.
- ❖ I am living in the new energy of myself,
  comfortably and easily.

We carry old energy patterns that influence our beliefs and behaviors not only from our birth experience but also from generational beliefs, unmet childhood needs, and any experience where we perceived that we were worthless or powerless.

Our first life experience was purposefully a struggle so we would be aligned with the consciousness of the planet to learn life's lessons through struggle and pain. We knew we had to know struggle to know what joy is. We live in a dimension of contrast. In order to know love, we had to create hate; in order to know good, we had to create evil; in order to know joy, we had to create pain. It is only through experiencing these contrasts that we can fully realize who we really are. In order to experience who we really are, we have had to experience who we are not. We are all pieces of God, just waiting to be awakened and fully realized.

We live in a time when we can easily and effortlessly clear away the old energies, beliefs, and patterns, and function completely in our new energy. My experience with energy psychology and energy medicine is that these new clearing therapies assist us in this accomplishing this.

At this time in which we live, clearing comes easily because the energy grids of the planet continue to release to allow us to live in a higher state of consciousness: knowing our true, core self. But it is hard for people to stay in the new energy vibration.

Humans are great creatures of habit and drama. I tell my clients that knowing and feeling your wholeness and true essence is natural but not familiar. What is familiar is your wounded state and dysfunctional life. You have become very good at staying alive in a life experience of pain and struggle. Overcoming pain and struggle has given you a sense of satisfaction and achievement, a false sense of security and love. Pain and struggle is not your natural state. If it were, you would not be coming to see me because you would feel highly satisfied with your life. You would be able to look at your life and say, "My life is all screwed up and I love it. I am completely satisfied."

You are not able to do that because it is very uncomfortable living a lie. As long as you continue living out these limited beliefs, you will feel dissatisfied. As you come to a remembrance and knowledge of your true essence, your god-self, it will not feel familiar and you will go back to the old way of being for a time. It is as if you have been living in a dark closet banging around. Clearing the limitations and old energy patterns will let you out of the closet. You will feel free and it may frighten you, so you will go back in the closet and continue to come out occasionally until you feel more and more comfortable. At some point you will close the door behind you and lock it, never to go in again, yet you will turn around and bang your head against the door just because it feels familiar. You'll say to yourself, *Oh pain—that feels right!* When you have experienced enough of that, you'll walk away from the closet to live a life of joy and happiness, co-creating with God.

CHAPTER 10

The Power and Purpose of Negative Emotion

There are two types of negative emotions. One is the negative feeling we generate from critical thoughts and beliefs about ourselves and the perceived worries we create about our lives. The second type is the uncomfortable feelings that are signals from our spirit and from God telling us that what we are currently thinking or the choices we are making are not in our highest good.

If you are still spending a lot of time feeling bad because you think you are not good enough, that you are less than others, *then just stop it!* Realize that you are wonderful, perfect, learning and growing, and doing the best you know how. You are worthwhile and important and making a great contribution to life just by being here. As long as you spend time feeling bad about yourself, or worrying about the past or the future, you are interfering with the real purpose of negative emotion. You are unable to use it as one of the best guidance systems you have.

By being in a place of feeling good, you are able to notice any negative feelings and use them as warning signals to guide and direct your life. The negative emotion is there to tell you that what you have your attention on is not really what you want and need.

When you start feeling negative, you have your thoughts on what you don't want and/or you are making choices that are leading you to what you don't want. Pay attention to the negative emotion. Stop and ask your spirit-self and God: *What am I currently thinking, believing, or choosing that is causing me to feel bad?*

Stay quiet and you will receive the answer. As you practice this more and more, you will receive your answers with more and more clarity. This knowledge will be accompanied by a distinct higher vibration that when continually honored will become more and more clear for you. If you ignore the negative emotion and keep doing what is causing you to feel bad, little by little you will subdue the powers of your spirit-self and the Holy Spirit from having an effect on you. You cut yourself off from your guidance system.

⌇

Steve was a worrier. He had patterns and beliefs about worry that kept him feeling bad most of the time. He believed that if he worried about his parents and brothers and sisters, they would know that he loved them. He believed that if he worried about his work, he would perform better in his duties. He believed that if he worried about potential problems in his life, he would be more prepared to deal with them when they showed up. He met a girl he fell in love with who was also a worrier. They married and within a few short months their lives were miserable. He worried about what she was thinking and feeling about him. He was constantly checking in with her for approval because he worried that his intentions and actions would not be okay with her. It wasn't long until he felt controlled by her and resentful of her, because he started to believe he had to check in with her, when it was really his own feelings of inadequacy that kept him in this pattern.

She worried that she had made the wrong decision in getting married and was not able to settle into the relationship because she wasn't even sure that being married was what she wanted. They were unable to support each other because they kept feeding each other's beliefs and patterns of worry. They were both so used to feeling bad and stressed out most of the time, that they were left to make decisions about their life without the power of their guidance system to direct them. Making decisions took a lot of effort, and they always worried that they weren't making the right ones.

Both Steve and his wife had experienced a lot of trauma in their childhood. They had both developed their patterns of worrying very early in their lives. As a result of their childhood traumas, they had deep beliefs that they could experience hurtful or painful experiences at any time without anyone protecting them. It is common that someone who has experienced a traumatic childhood believes, "I'll hurt myself before you can hurt me," and "There is always something bad going to happen to me so I might as well stay in a place of feeling bad—at least I can control it and it doesn't take me by surprise."

Worry is a self-inflicted way of controlling the hurt and disappointment. It creates a false sense of safety for people who believe something bad is always going to happen because they believe they can control their hurt and not be surprised by it any more.

Steve and his wife had great success clearing their inner-child fears and negative beliefs. In order to really experience a lasting change, they realized they had to change the way they perceived life and their pattern of worry. Once they understood the Law of Attraction, they were able to realize that their pattern of worry actually brought more upset into their lives. They are both committed to, and currently experiencing, a marriage wherein hope abounds and positive talk and feelings are the norm.

Being in a place of feeling good allows our negative emotions to play the role they were designed to play for us. God knew we would need a mechanism to give us clear and immediate feedback to guide our lives. When we are focusing on what is in our best interest and what creates more joy in our lives, we feel good. When we are focusing on what we don't want and that which will lead to more pain and upset, we feel bad. It is a simple formula that can be very, very accurate if we allow it to be fine-tuned and then use it.

Choose to feel good more and more of the time. The most important task you have every day is to stay in a place of feeling good. When we are in a place of feeling good we are in a high-frequency vibration that attracts more and more of what brings us joy. Your spirit-self knows the perfect plan for your life. All you have to do is stay in a place of feeling good to allow the plan to unfold effortlessly and continue to take form in your life.

$\mathcal{A}$FFIRMATIONS WORK

When you wake up in the morning and look in the mirror, do you say to yourself: *Hello, good-looking, it is good to see you again today. Thanks for being such a great person. I am grateful I am me and God loves and appreciates me?* Or do you look in the mirror and in your mind think, *Yuck!* And then do you lean a little closer to the mirror to more closely examine your perceived flaws? How do **you** start your day?

Tomorrow morning, go to the mirror and look into your eyes. Thank the person you see looking back at you for being there. Say out loud:

- ❖ I am grateful I am alive.
- ❖ I am honoring myself, and I am choosing to feel good today.
- ❖ I am a child of my Heavenly Father and Mother, and I am loved.

Even though Stuart Smalley on "Saturday Night Live" made speaking affirmations into a mirror look pretty stupid, the results can be very powerful. You will begin to feel better and your life will run more smoothly. When you start your day criticizing yourself, you initiate a low vibration and experience negative feelings. In this low vibratory state, you are emitting a signal that attracts more upsets and problems into your day. I often hear people say, "I am having a bad day," or, "It's just one of those days where everything goes wrong." In voicing these thoughts, we confirm that we have no power to change our experience. We believe that life is a series of random events and sometimes we have good days and frequently we have bad days.

"I am" are two of the most powerful words in our vocabulary. When we say, "I am," we are creating our present reality. By saying "I am" in reference to things we don't want in our life such as, "I am fat, I am overwhelmed, I am broke, I am frustrated, I am sick and tired, I am forgetful, I am worthless, I am stupid," we put our attention on the negative and create more of what we don't want. Our biology and life-forces hear us and respond accordingly. As we continue to focus on the "I am" negatives, we evoke negative feelings that send out a powerful signal that attracts back more of what we are giving attention to. The Universe is a big pool of energy waiting to be organized into our lives. We can have whatever we want. Put your attention on what you don't want, and that is what you will get. Put your attention on what you want, and that is what you will get.

We are the creators of our reality and "I am" are the two most powerful words with which to create. Christ refers to himself in Holy Scriptures as "the Great I Am."[9] He has said, "I am that I am," which means I am the creator. We are also creators. Use "I am" statements to create more of what you want.

A powerful process that can change our lives using "I

9 Doctrine and Covenants 38:1.

am" statements is called an energy circle. An energy circle is created by drawing an imaginary circle on the ground. Standing outside this imaginary circle, start speaking "I am" statements into the circle to create a hologram of energy. Let's say you want more abundance of health, happiness, positive relationships, money, and time. Draw the circle and, standing outside the circle, speak these statements out loud and throw them into the circle using your hands.

❖ I am grateful for my healthy body.

❖ I am experiencing my body as balanced and free of all disease.

❖ I am experiencing lots of energy and vitality.

❖ I am sleeping easily and I awake feeling refreshed and ready for a new day.

❖ I am thin and fit.

❖ I am grateful for the feelings of peace and well-being that abound in me.

❖ I am seeing the good in all of the events and details of my life.

❖ I am a positive person who enjoys the adventure of this life.

❖ I am creating more and more experiences that generate feelings of joy.

❖ I am attracting like-minded people with whom I love to interact.

❖ I am attracting people who are safe and respectful.

❖ I share myself easily and I am understood.

❖ I am experiencing my intimate relationships as blossoming and growing effortlessly.

❖ I am free of all debt.

❖ I am wealthy.

❖ I am successful.

❖ I am creating larger sums of money; money flows easily into my life.

❖ I am always flowing in more money than I am flowing out.

❖ I am comfortable with money, I spend it in integrity and have fun with it.

❖ I am generous in sharing my wealth because I always know there is plenty for others and me.

❖ I am experiencing that I have all the time I need.

❖ I move between the different activities of my day easily.

❖ I am always on time for my commitments.

❖ I am experiencing others as always on time for me.

❖ I flow easily within the structure of time in my day.

❖ I am grateful to be alive.

❖ I am creating more and more of what I want effortlessly.

❖ I am assisted by the powers and spirits of heaven. I ask for their help in all areas of my life. As I ask for what I want, they take care of orchestrating all the details and bring me what I have asked for. I am grateful for this powerful assistance.

After repeating these statements, step into the imaginary circle and the hologram of energy you have just created. Dress yourself in this energy by massaging it into your body from your toes up to your head. Open your arms, embrace this energy, and then close your arms over your heart. Then blow this energy out from your hands, as if you are casting the seeds of it into the ethers of the Universe to start forming and manifesting into your life.

As you practice this process daily, you will begin to see evidence of your affirmations develop in your life. As you are in the moment, notice that you are experiencing what you have asked for through your affirmations and complete the cycle of creation by offering out loud or in your heart a prayer of gratitude:

Thank you, God, for assisting me in my creation. I appreciate all the spirits who are helping me experience the full measure of my creative powers.

Mike and Karli are a married couple that were stuck in poverty consciousness. In their individual sessions, they became aware that they both came from generations who believed in not having enough. As they cleared their deeper beliefs, they were ready to create a different experience with money. They wanted to refinance their home. By refinancing at a lower rate, and maintaining the same mortgage amount, they would have money to pay off other debts.

They had attempted for several months to do this. Due to their poor credit history and current debt, they were repeatedly refused. I taught them to use energy circles with "I am" statements such as: "I am free of all past debt; I am comfortable with money; I am managing my money wisely; I am experiencing it is easy to get a new loan; I am experiencing a new loan coming easily and effortlessly to us." They had many of their own affirmations that they added. They committed to do this every day for a week.

By the end of the week, a loan officer, at a bank that had refused them previously, called them back. The loan officer said she was going through the applications and came upon theirs. She felt there was a way the bank could work with them. They set up an appointment to meet with her. The next time they saw me, they were very excited and encouraged. Within a few more weeks they had their new mortgage and were able to pay off other debts.

I have witnessed many clients' lives shifting into a positive momentum by just taking a few minutes each day to go through this process. Writing affirmations is also a powerful tool. When we speak these affirmations and evoke positive feelings as we step into the energy of them, we are truly creating our ideal reality.

The important thing to remember is that your thoughts are always creating your reality. It's up to you to be in charge of your thoughts, and consciously create a reality that is fulfilling. The alternative is a reality that is unconscious and haphazard. It's always your choice.

Complement your affirmations by starting your day positively. When you wake up, imagine your spiritual crew of angelic support is present in your room, waiting to meet with you. Ask them to assist you with the following:

- ❖ Bring me ideas of what I want.
- ❖ Help me connect with like-minded people.
- ❖ Help me be aware of my power.
- ❖ Help me be aware of my importance.
- ❖ Guide me to thoughts that are in harmony with my core desires.
- ❖ Bring me evidence of how this creation process works in fun, delightful, and comfortable ways.

By asking for this help, you will receive it. The heavens want to assist us in creating that which brings us more joy. They want us to be in a state of joy so we can move through our lives giving joy to more people.

Do not sit and wait for God to make your life better. The energy on the planet is the energy of partnering with the heavens. Set an intention to partner with God in creating a wonderful life, and you will experience the miracle of how quickly it can happen.

CHAPTER 12

PHYSICAL DISEASE HAS AN EMOTIONAL AND MENTAL ORIGIN

We are a creation of a tangible physical body and three subtle bodies. In addition to our physical body, which is visually obvious to all of us, we have a body of spirit, a mental body, and an emotional body. Our physical body is the only tangible body, because its vibration is the slowest. Our three other bodies exist as fields of higher vibratory energy around our physical body. These are fields around us that influence the health and wellness of our physical body.

These subtle bodies can carry disharmonies that have the power to break down our physical health. We can also carry in the physical body unexpressed, buried emotion and negative beliefs at a cellular level that have the power to deteriorate our body parts and functions. A healthy consciousness creates a healthy body; a negative consciousness deteriorates the body.

Many people do not consciously think the negative thoughts, and exhibit the negative mental patterns, that are commonly associated with their physical disease. They are optimistic people who have generally a good attitude about life. I have come to the conclusion that there are other ways to carry this negativity besides in our conscious, thinking mind. There may be inner-child parts that are still carrying unexpressed, buried emotion that has never been released. Beliefs that are very deep in the subconscious mind but are still active and disrupting the individual's good health.

The physical disharmony may be caused by generational beliefs and old karmic energies that have never been cleared. In any case, the body is a message center that keeps us alert and aware of more subtle parts of us that are not clear and balanced. By paying attention to what the body is trying to tell us, we can clear deeper beliefs of which we are not consciously aware.

Energy therapies clear the disharmonies and negative energy from their emotional/mental bodies, and from the deeper subconscious mind, which results in the body being more free to balance and heal itself.

Much has been written about the correlation of physical health and emotional and mental influences. Louise Hay has provided a very accurate and thorough compilation of physical diseases and their mental origin in her book *Heal Your Body*. I recommend it to everyone as a quick reference guide to assist you in discovering your negative patterns

Louise teaches: "The mental thought patterns that cause the most disease in the body are criticism, anger, resentment, and guilt. For instance, criticism indulged in long enough will often lead to diseases such as arthritis. Anger turns into things that boil and burn and infect the body. Resentment long-held festers and eats away all the self and ultimately can lead to tumors and cancer. Guilt always seeks punishment and leads to pain." [10] It is so much easier to release these negative emotional and mental patterns with the clearing technologies and healing arts we have

[10] Louise Hay. *Heal Your Body*. Carlsbad, CA: Hay House, Inc. 1982. pg. 7.

available to us today, when we are healthy, than to wait until we are in a physical crisis and our body has deteriorated considerably.

Many people have prevented what could have been great physical challenges in their lives because they listened and acted before the negative energies and patterns manifested as physical disease.

Our bodies have an agreement with us. They will let us know when we are out of balance. A physical imbalance is a message that there are emotional and mental disharmonies that need to be cleared. If you only try and fix the physical body without clearing the more subtle disharmonies, they will continue to reside and grow within you and manifest in another physical disease.

Clients have come to me after having been diagnosed with a condition, saying: "I am a diabetic," "I am a multiple personality," "I am attention deficit," "I have chronic fatigue," "I am overweight," "I am depressed," "I am a survivor of sexual abuse," "I am manic depressive," and many other physical, mental and emotional ailments. They have taken this diagnosis and made it part of their identity. By saying "I am" they are directing their body and all its cells, to confirm that this is my identity, so act accordingly.

We tell ourselves, everyone around us, and the Universe, who we think we are, which feeds more energy to our disharmonies and creates more of it. "I am" statements are the most powerful expression of telling our bodies what we believe our identity is. Remember, we control our minds, our minds control our bodies.

A healthy expression, one that supports us in overcoming disharmonies is, "My body has experienced the condition of _____ in the past, and now I choose to get the message it has for me, clear the disharmonies, claim my real self and move on." This statement accurately describes the situation without making it your current identity, puts it in the past, takes responsibility for clearing the disharmonies causing the imbalance, and exercises faith to heal.

WHY WE HOLD ON TO DISEASE AND DISHARMONY

Every dysfunction and disharmony we create has a hidden value to us. We have created it at a deeper level because we believe it is the only way we can make sure we have our needs met. We are usually unaware that we are getting value out of dysfunctional patterns because the payback is hidden from our conscious mind. When we become aware of the value these patterns give us, we are then free to let them go and meet our needs in healthy ways.

Kathy had been diagnosed with chronic fatigue. In just a few sessions she discovered she had a belief that she was not lovable unless she was doing something to make her feel worthwhile. She was a classic overachiever and did not know how to give herself a break. There was a Little Kathy inside her that believed she did not measure up and could never do anything well enough. She had to keep trying with no rest. Her chronic fatigue condition was what she created to give herself permission to let go and take a break. She needed the condition because she was unable to give herself this permission without it.

In her sessions, she easily cleared the old emotions and beliefs, formed new ones, and changed her behavior patterns—taking time to sit and meditate each day. She verbally acknowledged her self-worth, vitality, and energy. She now holds the belief, *I am worthwhile and loved, I choose to do what is inspired action in my life. All that I do is good enough, and I am experiencing other people knowing that about me.*

Andrea had been experiencing many years of bad health. Nothing very dramatic, she was just always getting sick. In her sessions she discovered that when she was a little girl, she received a little more attention when she was ill. We worked with a five-year-old part of her that did not want to give up being sick. In fact it was the five-year-old's job to attract illnesses just so Andrea would receive love and support. In her adult life there was always a doctor or nurse who would listen to her and want to help her feel better.

Andrea believed that without the illnesses she might not get any love and attention. Like many others I have worked with, her deepest fear was that she might discover that she was really inferior and inadequate and no one would want to love her. With this possibility in her deeper mind she was afraid to let go of the substitute she had created. I said to her, "So you think if we go deep within you, I am going to discover the real truth about you which would sound something like this: 'I am sorry, Andrea, but it seems you really are inadequate and unlovable. You did come into this life less than everyone else, there is nothing I can do for you. Good luck as you continue to survive as a lesser human being with a flawed spirit!'"

When they hear their deepest fears expressed, people usually realize how ridiculous their fears are and have a good laugh. They begin to trust that as we start clearing away the layers of lies, they will find a love for themselves that will bring them to their knees in gratitude. Many clients begin to feel this self-love in their first session.

In my early forties, I discovered a substantial lump in my breast. I told my husband and asked him not to make a big deal about it. I went to the doctor and she told me I should get a mammogram within the week. I made the decision at this point that I was not going to tell anyone because I did not want attention put on the worst-case scenario. I was also aware a part of me thought it would be nice to get a lot of attention and concern from others. So, I told no one, and proceeded instead to understand my emotional/mental relationship to this disharmony.

I learned that breast lumps were generated from fear of letting go of your children, over-mothering patterns and overbearing attitudes as a parent. I certainly did not like to think of myself this way. Rather than resist it, I accepted the possibility that this was my stuff, and asked God to let me know how to change this.

I noticed that my oldest daughter was beginning to date, and maybe I was a little too emotionally involved. Therapists can be overbearing with their children, because they think they are helping them with so many answers. I was willing to change all that. I thanked my body for the message and started a new thought pattern that sounded like this: "I am perfect just as God created me. I believe I am important and I make a difference. I know when to speak and when to keep quiet. I am allowing my children to be who they are. We are all safe and free."

The first mammogram identified the lump as either a tumor or a cyst. Another test identified it as a benign cyst. My doctor encouraged me to have it surgically removed. My appointment with a surgeon was six weeks after the mammogram. During that time I did visualizations, imagining white laser light clearing out the cyst. I continued repeating my new beliefs and noticed when I was overbearing with my children and stopped myself. When I went for my appointment with the surgeon, the cyst was gone.

This was my first experience with a physical condition of this kind since I have been a very healthy person. I know many people have healed their bodies of more than my little cyst.

I am grateful for the agency we have to choose to heal our bodies, I recognize that not everyone is meant to heal their physical diseases. Some are meant to move on to the spirit world. My father-in-law passed away many years ago. He had cancer and a bleeding ulcer at the time of his passing. He was a very prominent leader in his church and several thousand of the church's members knew of his condition and were praying for him. Shortly before his passing, he knelt in private prayer and asked God if the blessings from the prayers that were being given for him were his to do with whatever he desired, and he asked that they be distributed to family members and others who needed them more. He took the literal power of prayer and asked that the healing energy be made available to others because he knew that his mortal experience was complete. There have been many times when family members have felt the force of those prayers affect and bless our lives.

If you are suffering with physical ailments, find the emotional and mental origin of them. You will experience increased results and more powers of healing at the physical level as you let go of your repressed negative emotions and limiting beliefs.

Use your faith to receive the gift of healing and you will receive it, if it is a part of your divine plan to heal. If it is your time to move on to spirit, come to terms with this and go in peace. Either way, using your profound spiritual powers will help you move more gracefully and easily into your next segment of existence. All is well.

CHAPTER 14

ENERGY HEALING FOR DEPRESSION

This is my simplified definition of depression: a state of feeling "bad" most or all of the time. It is the experience of being in a vibration of very low, uncomfortable energy that offers little or no relief.

At the finest levels of our being—our quantum self—we are all energy. Subtle energies that are unseen to the eye (by most people) vibrate within us and around us constantly. Depression is a very uncomfortable energy state to exist in. It is so uncomfortable because it contradicts the truth of who we are and who God created us to be. God created us to be in a state of joy. We are literally hard-wired for joy.

The good news about depression is that it is not who you really are. Your depression is not your identity: it is your experience. It is an energy experience that has taken hold of your life. Since it is not your identity, you can change it. However, it may require doing some energy work and clearing of limiting beliefs, both conscious and subconscious, to allow you to feel better.

The subconscious limiting beliefs held within your being feed the negative energy you are experiencing. Your conscious negative thoughts continue to feed this negative energy. Most people suffering from depression have a tendency towards negative thinking. They assume that if they *feel* bad, they must *be* bad.

You are always free to choose whatever thoughts you want. Even if you are processing some uncomfortable negative energy, you are always free to think a positive thought. It is appropriate when a lot of emotion is coming up to say to yourself, *I am clearing this negative energy. It is no longer serving me to experience this in my life.*

Thoughts create; therefore, whatever you believe in, you will experience. Since energy follows thought, create thoughts of wellness and you will create an energy of wellness that will be fed to your being.

I have worked with numerous clients who have a hidden motivation or need for their depression. We need our illness when we believe it is keeping us safe from something we fear. Depression becomes a good friend that is always there when you need it. It sticks by us and keeps us safe from the unpredictable risks in the world.

If you have been depressed for a long time, your body is now convinced that feeling depressed is what being alive feels like. Without the depression, your body may think it is going to die. With the use of your mind and your faith, you can retrain your body to operate at a higher frequency of energy so it can once again know itself in light and truth.

Consider the possibility that the origin of much of your depression is connected to your birth. If your mother was anxious, depressed, worried, or troubled during your gestation, you took on all that energy in the earliest formation of yourself. Most people are walking around still carrying and trying to process out their birth energy. If you had a complicated gestation or delivery, you were hit from the very beginning with some big negatives that were imprinted in your psyche.

From personal experience, and from working with hundreds of clients, I have come to the conclusion that there is a generational pattern of depression for most people. You can trace depression back in my family line for several generations. I believe most people who are dealing with painful life experiences are playing a role in healing their generation and breaking family patterns. If your great-grandma never addressed her negative emotions and they never were cleared, that energy and information has been passed on to you in the genetics of your family. You can clear what your body holds at a cellular level so you can heal yourself and clear the pattern of depression from your family.

A Process to Clear Your Generational Depression

Imagine yourself standing in the light with a higher power (Jesus Christ, angels, God, or Holy Spirit). Ask your generations that have lived before you to come into the light. Imagine all these people in the light with you. Ask your higher self of all the depression you have experienced, how much of it is generational and how much is your own. You will get two numbers that equal 100 percent. For most people the generational percent is more than 50 percent and their part is less than 50 percent. It is usually 70/30 or 80/20. Tell your ancestors you are choosing to clear this pattern from the family.

Draw a picture of a garbage can on a sketchpad. Place the pattern of depression—with all the negative beliefs and emotions that you have experienced with it—into the garbage can. When this is all in the garbage can, enlarge the picture of the garbage can as big as you can imagine it. Look at it as an observer and say, *It's just energy. I am not in the picture. I am the one looking at the picture.* Now create a blowtorch in your mind, set your picture on fire, and watch it burn into ashes. Take the ashes and spread them on the ground. Watch beautiful flowers grow up through the ashes returning life-giving energy to you and your ancestors. Imagine every cell in your body being filled with life-giving energy. How does that feel? Imagine your ancestors cheering for you and congratulating you on your choosing to clear this pattern.

You *can* heal. I believe that whatever we are challenged by in our lives, God gave us the mechanism within us to heal it. There is literally a blueprint for healing held in your DNA that has all the information your mind and body needs to heal. I believe that we created illness to teach us the capacity we have to exist in difficult states and to turn us to a higher power to seek help.

Calling upon Christ's energy or the energy of the heavens activates the healing powers that lie dormant within us. As you put your attention on light and truth, light and truth awakens within you. Don't wait until you feel better to think well. Your mind is a higher power than your emotions. Your mind can raise the vibration of your emotional state as you clear away the lies and illusions you carry and call forth the truth of the person God created you to be. You can create whatever you want with your life. The God I believe in did not cast us down here to live in a state of despair or to die in that state. I believe he guaranteed our ability to succeed by endowing us with all that we need to create success. For most people, being depressed is familiar. Feeling good is not. Often we choose what is familiar over what feels good because we know how to exist there and it feels safe.

We live at a time on this planet when it is becoming increasingly more difficult to stay depressed. It will require more work to stay in depression than to heal it. The real challenge for us as humans is no longer "How much can we suffer?" It is "How much joy can we hold and how long can we hold it?" Consider the possibility that you chose and created your experience of depression just to see yourself overcome it. As big as you have known depression is as big as you can now know joy. Choose to become one of God's miracles and clear and heal what is no longer serving you. God bless you. I know you can do it.

CHAPTER 15

HEALING CAN HAPPEN QUICKLY

We have been given the power to heal our lives instantly. Energy follows thought, and since we are, at the finest levels of creation, a system of energy, our thoughts can heal us. Our faith is what determines how quickly this can occur. During Jesus Christ's ministry, he healed many people. The one healing that allowed me to consider how quickly we can heal, is the story of the woman who touched his garment and was healed immediately. Christ was among a multitude of people when a woman approached him from behind. She had been trying to heal a bleeding problem for twelve years. She had spent all her money on physicians, yet had not been healed. She approached Christ from behind, touched the border of his garment, and her bleeding immediately ceased. Christ felt energy leave his system and asked who had touched him. Peter, one of his disciples, was surprised by this comment because people were thronging all around and pressing in on him.

He asked Christ, "Master, the multitude throng thee and press thee, and sayest thou, Who touched me?"

And Jesus said, "Somebody hath touched me: for I perceive that virtue is gone out of me."[11]

---

[11] Luke 8:45-46.

Christ knew that the vibration within himself, which he offered to others, restored their systems to wholeness. He offered it freely and still does to anyone who has the faith. In the case of this woman, she knew Christ had discovered her, so she came trembling and fell down before him. She told Christ and all those who were present why she had touched him and how she was healed immediately.

Christ said to her, "Daughter, be of good comfort: thy faith hath made thee whole; go in peace."[12]

He told her that it was her faith that had made her whole, not, "I have made thee whole." She called the healing forth through her desire and faith that she could be healed, and she was healed immediately. Her system of energy remembered its whole, perfect state in the presence of Christ's energy. Christ's blueprints of wholeness activated her blueprints of wholeness on all levels, and she was restored.

I believe Christ and his energy works through the healers of today.

He told us, "He that believeth on me, the works that I do shall he do also; and greater works than these shall he do."[13]

What is Christ suggesting? Does this mean he believes I can assist people in healing immediately and that I have the potential to influence even greater miracles than he did? I asked God and Christ about this, and they reassured me that it means exactly what it says.

Christ isn't physically here right now, and I am. It is only because of him that this is possible. My faith as a healer, matched with his power of healing, combined with the faith of the person being healed, will create miracles—immediate healing.

[12] Luke 8:48.
[13] John 14:12.

We live in a time when this healing is more and more available. As the vibration of the earth continues to increase and more of Christ's energy is released into our physical realm, the more power we have to experience this. Remembering, being restored to our wholeness, and owning our spiritual identity can be a graceful and comfortable experience. We no longer need to work and struggle in a long, arduous journey.

In the last fifty years, we have pioneered the emotional, mental, and spiritual plains of our existence. Our ancestors pioneered the physical plains. They pioneered the land, built communities, and developed technologies to free us to pioneer and clear the remaining aspects of ourselves. Many people have pioneered and cleared the emotional and mental plains to pave a way for us to move easily into our spiritual purpose.

I tell my clients that in the physical world you no longer have to walk across the United States pushing a handcart to get to the other side. You can hop on a jet plane and fly there in a few hours. You can still choose the walk if you prefer to experience the struggle, or you can relax in a seat, be served drinks and a meal, and even be entertained by a movie as you travel.

It is the same with moving into your spiritual purpose and identity. You can struggle to get there and take years, or you can just be there. What used to take months and even years to cross the physical plains, now takes a few hours. What used to take years to clear the emotional and mental planes to come to your spiritual truth, can happen as quickly as you can believe it.

Once you've felt the vibration of your spiritual identity, the key to staying in it is keeping that vibration constant. What keeps you from maintaining your spiritual vibration, your spirit-self, constantly, is the baggage that you carry at the subconscious, cellular level of yourself and in the energy field around you.

I assist clients in clearing what used to take them years to clear on their own. RET and energy therapies are like the modern-day jet plane: they are a resource in helping you get to where you want to be faster. Once you arrive, you realize you have always been there, you just had debris that kept you from seeing it.

RET is not the healing power; it is a clearing technology that stimulates your mind, body, and psyche's own natural clearing mechanism. As clearing occurs in a session, low vibratory energy is released, and Christ Light—a higher vibratory energy—is restored and healing occurs.

Healing is the experience of being restored to your spirit truth in the physical body. The higher the vibration you can hold, the more potent and powerful your faith.

I believe that which is of God is light, and that when we make choices that align us with God we receive more light. That light within us grows brighter and brighter as we continue to make choices to follow God and to be useful to ourselves and others in our spiritual purpose.

☀

CHAPTER 16

RECEIVE YOUR HEALING NOW

What did Christ always ask the person he was about to heal? He always asked in some fashion, "Do you believe?" He was asking, "Do you have the faith to be healed?" A common response was "Yes, Lord." Once they responded in faith, Christ flowed healing energies to them, they received these healing powers and manifested immediate healing.

In at least one instance, the gentleman that was seeking a healing from Christ did not have the faith. Because he lacked the belief that he could be healed, he asked for something else. What he asked for is something we could all be asking for in our lives. He asked, "Lord, I believe; help thou my unbelief." He knew his faith was a prerequisite of the healing occurring. Since his faith did not match his desire, he asked Christ to bless him with an increase in his belief so he could receive the healing.

We are free to ask for this assistance with any of our desires. If our function of desiring, asking, and believing is what controls the flow of getting what we ask for, not believing is where we fall short. Ask God to bless your belief so you can receive what you have asked for. If you are asking to be healed, know that in the asking, you activate the giving. Christ withholds his healing powers from no one. We withhold ourselves from receiving it when we do not have the belief that it is possible.

We have made it very difficult to get well in our culture. Very few people believe in immediate healing. We have set into place a process that requires a lot of time, money, drugs, and research to receive healing.

Consider the possibility that if you have asked to be healed, it has been given. If you are not experiencing the results of being healed, you are out of alignment with the healing. Your thoughts, language, and reference to still not being healed keep you from experiencing yourself as being healed.

There is a healing in place for everyone. That healing can look like coming into full wellness or being released from this physical realm. *Desire* to be healed, ask Christ to heal you, *believe* you will be healed, and *receive* your healing now.

THE EARTH HAS A SOUL AND IS CHANGING

Mother Earth is a living being. She is a life force with a spiritual purpose and mission. She is changing, as are we, her inhabitants. Research has shown that the magnetic grids are continually decreasing and the vibrational frequency is increasing. The earth has agreements with mankind to keep us from getting stuck. We are meant to continue to spiritually grow and evolve. As the physics of the planet change, we are forced to look at our lives and make changes as well.

This is affecting us by making us more powerful in our thoughts and feelings. Whatever intention we put out, whether positive or negative, the results are coming into our lives faster and more amplified. If your focus is on the negative, then you will experience life as getting harder. If your focus is on the positive, you will experience life as getting easier. Whatever negative patterns you are creating in your life, you will find it increasingly more and more uncomfortable to stay in them.

The good news is it has never been easier to make changes. As the vibration of the planet increases, we are dwelling in more light and truth. As we make changes that bring us into more light, that light is in harmony with the space wherein we exist. More light is added upon us and we are able to stabilize these positive changes more quickly. We are less likely to slip into old negative patterns as we continue to set our intentions daily to stay in the new energy.

Some people notice the energy shifts as they occur. Even if you are not consciously aware of these shifts, they are biologically affecting you. There are days you will feel disoriented, tired, and lethargic. It may be hard to stay focused and productive. You seem to require more or less sleep than usual. Eating patterns can change and digestive processes can be thrown off.

If we were more conscious of these changes and were honest with each other, you would hear people saying, "I'm a little out of balance today due to the big shift the planet is going through this week. If I seem a little edgy, just ignore it. It's not your fault, it's the magnetic grids dropping."

We also wouldn't judge ourselves so harshly for feeling tired and worn out because we would honor that our bodies needed more rest to acclimate to the changes and get back into balance.

The earth is changing to benefit us. As we choose to change with it, we will increase well-being in all aspects of our lives.

CHAPTER 18

We Can Change the Way We Feel Instantly

Why don't we feel good all the time? Most people believe that we can't, that we are subject to the whims of our emotions, and have to learn to make it through the random hard times of life. In our society, we have a strong belief that there are some days we are not going to feel good and we just have to suffer through them.

It is socially unacceptable to claim you feel good all of the time, or that at least you have figured out how to. Most people do not believe you and think you are in denial of all your life's problems. Others dismiss you as an emotional, upper-class snob who is no longer willing to play the game of emotional duress.

Once you've made the decision to take charge of your life and how you feel, choosing to take accountability for when you feel bad and changing it to feeling good, you will find yourself in fewer and fewer conversations with a negative focus. Many of your relationships change because the people in your life that you attracted to lick your wounds while you lick theirs are not always as eager to give up their pity parties and their victim experience.

That's okay. This gives you the opportunity to let go and allow, showing unconditional love for others, and saying to yourself, *I guess that person wants more of that experience. I am here for them when they are ready to change it.*

I remember sitting in a Sunday school lesson when the teacher asked the class, "Who feels good all the time?" I weakly half-raised my hand so that only the person next to me could see it. She turned to me and said, "Oh, you do not, nobody does." I replied, "Well, I'm working on it. I believe it's possible."

The teacher's point was that nobody could feel good all the time so we were going to learn how to better survive the hard times. I would have preferred a lesson on the powers we have to feel good all of the time—independent of others' choices. Each of us has the freedom to choose perceptions of our life experiences and the world around us that support us in feeling good all the time. Each of us has the power to change how we feel instantly.

As a society, we have a collective belief that there are certain life events that will cause us to feel bad. In fact, if we felt good about them, we would be looked down upon as behaving inappropriately and demonstrating that we are apathetic or insensitive.

Let's take the experience of death. When a loved one or someone close to us passes on from the physical realm to return to spirit, it is common to feel a tremendous loss and to grieve this loss. However, the reference point that the person died implies they are dead to us and are gone for good. We usually feel a variety of emotions from anger to sadness to confusion, amongst many others, including peace. Our perception of this experience dictates how we end up feeling. If we change our perception, we can change how we feel.

Sue had been grieving the sudden death of her young son for nearly two years by the time she came in to see me. She was stuck in a deep grief and in many ways she had died along with him. The rest of her family was experiencing not only the death of the boy, but also the loss of their wife and mother to grief and despair. She believed that she could not be happy with him gone. Her perception was that it should never have happened and she was very angry with God for taking her son away from her. She was committed to her beliefs and was not willing to consider another way of looking at it—a way that could bless her life rather than destroy it. She hungered for a witness from her son that he was okay and that he was near her. Every time something happened to remind her of her son, she focused on his absence. It did not occur to her to think that the reminders occurred because he was making a connection with her to let her know he was okay and close by.

I really wanted a miracle for her, yet my wanting it is not always enough. I believe I can ask for miracles for others and they will be given, yet the person will not always notice the miracle they have been given because their focus is on what they don't have. The miracle comes and goes unnoticed by them.

In Sue's case, we attempted to clear the feelings of deep grief and sadness. We cleared a lot of beliefs like: *My heart aches. I am broken-hearted. I feel empty inside.*

I don't know how I can go on with all this pain. I am scared. I loved him so. The future is bleak without him. I want to die. I am helpless over the situation and angry with God. I must have done something to deserve this. I feel like I lost a part of myself.

After we cleared these negative feelings, we reframed with a lot of positive beliefs like: *Thank you, God. I am healed. I am at peace with my life. My heart is whole and healed. I trust that all my experiences in my life are purposeful. I am grateful for the gifts my loved ones have shared with me. I am protected and nurtured. I am connected and communicating with the ones I love in all dimensions. I trust God to support me.*

Sue was a wealthy and powerful woman. Her need for control propelled her to the top of her industry. Often, people who are addicted to power and control typically have a wounded inner-child state that they have completely hidden from themselves because they never want to revisit the sense of threat and powerlessness they experienced as children. In Sue's case, she had worked hard to get into a position of power and control so she could never be hurt by anyone again.

Although the death of her son was a tremendous gift, she could not see it as that.

Sue was attached to her perception. She was so angry because she felt so powerless. The event of her son's passing was the one thing in her life she could not control with her money and her high-powered position. That is why it was a perfect gift for her. It was perfect because it triggered her deep reservoir of beliefs and feelings of powerlessness that she had worked so hard to cover up throughout her life. If she had acknowledged that an inner-child part of her still carried the beliefs and feelings of powerlessness and fear, she could have cleared them and easily been restored to her true essence. She could have created a new belief such as: "I am loved and I am powerful in a healthy spiritual way. I am grateful for the experience of my son returning to spirit so I could reclaim the truth of who I am. I am creating a relation-ship and communication with him of a spiritual nature, different yet more wonderful from the physical one we knew before. I am close to him and feel his comforting presence often. I know he still loves me. I am helping others with similar experiences to come to a place of peace and connection with their loved ones who have passed on." If we can see the gift of each experience offered to us in this lifetime, we can receive it and then take our awareness and share it with others so they can receive their gifts, too.

Until Sue was willing to clear and change her neg-ative beliefs and perceptions, she would be stuck in her pain. At the time I worked with her, she was very committed to dying with her anger intact so she could take it back to God and say, "See what you did to me?" She thought she needed evidence to prove to God that her son's death was wrong and God was to blame. But God loves us so much, and wants us to have the full experience of our agency and power, that he is even willing to be the "bad guy" for us when we are unwilling to see it any other way.

The gift was that her son was willing to sacrifice his life to assist her in coming into touch with the fears and insecurities that were buried so deeply she had forgotten she had them. She needed an event of this magnitude to remind her she was not on this earth just to make money, that her real purpose was to come through the dark night of her soul and bring her higher spiritual self into her day-to-day life. Her son loved her so much, he was willing to play this part for her.

⁓

Sue is one of the few clients I have worked with over the years who did not get as far along in her process as I had hoped. I am reminded when this occurs that it is not my job to heal people or be responsible for waking them up to the truth that resides within them. Ultimately it is each individual's choice. I know that once they have chosen to allow the solutions to their life's challenges to be awakened within themselves, I can assist them to do it with more grace and ease. When I meet someone who is not ready to make that choice, I can create a feeling of peace by telling myself, *Everything is perfect; God loves all of us. I choose to see this person lovingly and accept that they still need more of their current experience.* I turn them over to God and notice that I want to attract people who are ready to heal and not just looking for sympathy or relief.

The next time you are feeling stuck in a place of feeling bad, ask God to bless you with an understanding and a perception of your experience that will invite and awaken peaceful soothing feelings inside of you. Be willing to clear the negative beliefs and feelings by asking to have these cleared from the deepest parts of your cells.

The words of this prayer could sound like this:

Thank you, God, for blessing me with a perception of my current experience that supports me in feeling good. I ask that through the power of Christ's atonement all my cells will be cleared of the negative beliefs and feelings that are keeping me stuck in this perception. This I ask in the name of Jesus Christ, amen.

Be willing to support yourself in feeling good more and more of the time, and you will be gifted with the rare art of being in charge of your feelings and feeling good in any circumstance. Remember that feeling good does not just mean feeling happy. Feeling good consists of a myriad of feelings that can include even grief. The difference is that in the process of grief, you feel a sustaining energy of peace and tranquility offered to you by the Holy Spirit to carry you through what may seem at first a difficult experience. At some point you will have the insight to claim the gifts in the changes that are occurring and to return to a place of balance with more light and truth than you had before.

THE UNIVERSE ALWAYS HOLDS US ACCOUNTABLE

⟣⟢

There is always an opportunity given to us if we are willing to be consciously accountable for our choices. Because of the Law of Attraction, we are the sole creators of our life experience. The cause is created by the choice, and the result is the effect. Our response to this formula is accountability.

In difficult or painful experiences, we may find it hard to take ownership and we blame others or forces beyond our control. We want to believe, *I couldn't have created that!* We may get away with fooling ourselves and the external world that it was not our fault or our responsibility, yet we will never fool the Universe and we will be held accountable.

We are held accountable energetically. If we lie, steal, control, hurt others, deceive, cheat, hurt ourselves, ignore our own needs and behave in a manner that is not Christ-like to ourselves or others, we lose vital energy that sustains our health and well-being. Every choice we make either drains our spirit or fuels our spirit. What fuels our spirit fuels our body. What drains our spirit drains our body. The accountability of our choices does not always seem obvious to us. Many people suffer from poor health, need, dissatisfaction, and unhappiness in life because of their patterns of blame, control, denial, and their unwillingness to take ownership for their creations. For a good overview in more detail of this dynamic see *Anatomy of the Spirit* by Caroline Myss.[14]

Even though it appears that some people get away with wrongdoing, at some level they are held accountable for their choices. If you find it hard to admit to yourself what you perceive as mistakes in your life, change your perception from seeing it as a mistake and relabel it a learning experience. Your role in accountability is to learn from your choices and choose again with more integrity.

Most people have patterns of thought and behavior that are not serving them. My professional role is to help them identify these patterns that for some have been with them most of their life. As long as they keep blaming outside experiences and other people, they are powerless to change anything. Their opportunity is to see their role in the pattern, why they keep creating it, and how the Universe holds them accountable. When you can do this with every aspect of your life, you will be in deliberate control over your life experience.

Many of our beliefs were established in childhood. Patterns were created to keep us alive and created a sense of safety and importance in our world. As adults we can identify those beliefs and patterns and say, "This kept me alive when I was five years old, but I don't need it now."

⌣⌐

Frank had been out of work for nearly five years. He had worked on and off for brief periods during that time. He had also attempted to start his own company

[14] Caroline Myss. *Anatomy of the Spirit.* New York, NY: Three Rivers Press. 1996.

and was still working at this when we met.

He came from a family where the men struggled to make ends meet. Work never came easy for his grandfather and great-grandfather. Both had been unemployed off and on throughout their adult lives. By the end of his twelve-session program, Frank felt clearer and was motivated to create his own successful business.

After several months he returned to see me. He was further in debt and no further along in his business growth. I took him through a process called the "Circle of Creation" that supports people in taking ownership of their life experiences. He claimed he had done everything he knew to make it work, both spiritually and temporally, and was feeling very angry and discouraged.

By the end of the process, Frank came to a core realization that was still keeping him stuck. Several years earlier, Frank had a job that he felt good about and secure in. His wife was given a promotion that required a move to a different state. Frank left his work to support her.

After they moved, his wife only stayed at this position a short time, quitting to be home full-time as a mother.

Frank had a strong pattern of blaming others, particularly his wife and former bosses. What Frank realized was that he had a hidden belief that his wife took him from his perfect job and it was her fault he was unhappy. At a subconscious level a wounded part of Frank held the core belief: *Others have power over me and I can never have what I want.* This part of him was resentful towards his wife and wanted to punish her. The best way to punish her was to not make any money because she suffered from this, too. If he made money, she would be provided for and never have to pay a price for making him leave his job.

As long as Frank projected this power on his wife, he was a victim to her. When he realized what he really wanted, he successfully cleared the anger and resentment towards his wife. Frank was then free to be in harmony with his new belief, that he was capable and worthy of attracting a wonderful job experience into his life.

Once Frank took ownership of his choice to leave and support his wife in moving, he had his power back to direct to what he really wanted. As long as he had a hidden value in not working—getting back at his wife who he believed messed up his life, Frank was powerless to create what he really wanted. Frank came to understand that his wife was just playing a role for him to support him in learning the lessons of choice, accountability and forgiveness. Within the month Frank attracted a position with the company he had left several years earlier, a position that had just opened up that month. He was able to stay in the same place in a position he enjoyed even more.

By choosing to be accountable and taking ownership of everything you experience, you will really have the power to create a wonderful life. In this process of ownership and self-referral, choose to leave out the self-judgment and criticism. That just creates feelings of worthlessness and guilt, which are very disabling.

Our spirits fully understand we came to earth to gain experience. We learn more and more clearly what we do want as a byproduct of experiencing what we don't want. The next time you have an experience you don't want, ask yourself what you *do* want and start creating it. Tell the Universe what you want and your spiritual crew will immediately go to work to bring it to you.

.

Everything We Experience Outside Ourselves Is Just a Mirror for Us

One morning a client called me and asked: "Do you believe that the people and experiences in our lives are a mirror to us, telling us what we really believe about ourselves?" I asked her what she thought when she asked herself the same question. She said she didn't know because she was confused. She shared that since she had last seen me, she had gotten back together with the boyfriend with whom she had broken an engagement a few months earlier. The last session she had with me was focused on clearing the beliefs that kept her recreating the pattern of settling for men that did not have the same spiritual ambitions and desires she did.

She explained to me that she had gone back to him because she felt emotionally empty without him and when she was with him she felt good. When they were apart, she had tremendous doubt and emotional discomfort. All of this was very confusing to her.

Everything we experience in the external world is a mirror. Our conscious thoughts and feelings, and more importantly, our subconscious thoughts and feelings, send out a signal to the world to attract into our lives exactly what we believe about ourselves. If we want to know what we really believe about ourselves, all we have to do is look at the experience of our lives. Whatever we are experiencing is what we are believing. Life is a mirror for us to get the feedback about what we are believing that we are too often unwilling to seek on our own.

When something negative happens to me, I ask myself: *What am I still believing about myself that would attract this into my life?* If I have uncomfortable feelings and yet I am not tuning in to what wants to be corrected in my life, I ask the question: *Why am I feeling these negative feelings? What am I to notice about my life and make different?*

If I am willing to accept the answers, I am given the information that will support me in making corrections that will create more and more of what brings me real joy and happiness.

My client asked me: "Then why do I feel happy when I am with him, and feel doubt when I am not?" I suggested that she may still be believing that she has unmet emotional needs that he can fill for her. Therefore, when she is with him she feels more whole and complete. When she is not with him her guidance system is trying to send her a message that this is not in her highest good. The negative emotion is a signal for her to pay attention to because there is someone out there she would be happier with. She admitted that he did not have the same spiritual ambitions and desires as she did and that their connection was strongly physical and emotional and lacked the spirituality she was so committed to in her life. Her rationale was that in time this could change and maybe it was that way so she could learn unconditional love. She was not comfortable sharing her spiritual experiences and insights with him because he was not open to that.

I had suggested in earlier sessions that if she could believe it was possible, there was a man out there that she could create a deep and honoring partnership with—including the physical, emotional, mental, and spiritual connections she was seeking. It was her opportunity to look at who she had attracted into her life. Was she settling for less? It all depended on what she wanted to experience. If she were completely satisfied with her relationship with him, and it was what she really wanted, she wouldn't have the doubts and confusion. If she believed she deserved to have a man in her life that was like-minded and wanted the same things she wanted, the man in her life would change and show up in a manner to reflect that back to her. Or he would drop out of her life and a man that matched her belief—*I am loved and supported by a man that loves and honors his spirituality and mine*—would show up in her life. It comes down to: "What do you want to create, and what do you want to experience?"

In viewing life as a mirror, we are able to see what we believe at a deeper level, things our emotions and conscious mind distort and keep hidden from us. When we let our emotions rule our lives, we are easily drawn into relationships and experiences that are dishonoring to who we truly are. When we let our rational conscious thinking mind rule our lives, we have to see the evidence before we believe something, which stifles our faith. When our physical body rules our lives, we are subject to addictions and appetites of the flesh. All these states keep our spirit, our soul essence, from being the most dominant influence in our lives.

When we allow our spirit, which is connected to Christ, to direct our lives, we are willing to surrender our emotions, our conscious thinking mind, and our appetites and physical passions to it. In this surrendering we subject our will to our spirit's will.

Our spirit's will is always aligned with God's will for us. It is in this state of being that we are truly aligned with Christ-energy and every thought, feeling, and physical desire is in harmony with God. It is in this state that we attract like-minded people and experiences that bring us joy. Life mirrors back to us a life of well-being and harmony wherein all things that are good and desired can come effortlessly.

CHAPTER 21

Your Energy Speaks Louder Than Your Words

The next time you want to influence someone to change, stop talking and offer them your loving energy instead. Notice the power you have to shift the energy that is flowing between you and your ability to influence people changing because of the loving energy you're flowing.

When someone has not asked you for your feedback and you give it anyway, their defenses are triggered and very little of what you are sharing is received. One of the more common questions I am asked at my seminars is, "What can I do or say to help so-and-so get it?" Or, "How can I get so-and-so to want to heal?"

I always respond with, "Say and do nothing." It is not your job to get others to heal. Healing and choosing to change for the better can only be successful if the individual is wanting it and asking for it.

In staying quiet, you can now hold your friend or loved one in the image of wanting to change and heal. Whatever perception you hold of people, you flow that energy to them. You give them an energy offering.

Whatever that offering is supports them in creating more of it. That is the support you are giving them.

I think of God as only able to perceive us in the truth He created for us. He never buys into the lies and illusions we hold about ourselves. In His perception of seeing us in our truth, He flows a constant energy to us. Through His grace, that continues to support us in manifesting ourselves as that truth. That is His unconditionally loving character. How many people in our lives do we hold in that way? We look at all the evidence people give us, and base our perception of who they are on that evidence. I am grateful that God does not use my life experience in His determination of who I am. I am grateful that He continues to hold me in the light and truth He created for me.

It is my opportunity to have a god-like perception of others, especially my husband and children. Our family members are usually the people we seem to have the most ability to hold in limiting views. To perceive my husband and children as god-like allows me to flow an energy of unconditional love to them and offers them the most powerful support I have to give.

Your energy offering has more power to influence someone's life turning for the good than anything you could say to influence that. As you support people with flowing them this positive, loving energy, they often show up wanting to learn more about what you know and even asking for your help. Hold an intention for them to come to you seeking and asking. It is only when people ask that they are truly open to receiving what you have to share. We are very powerful in behalf of each other, either adding to our growth or stifling it, depending on the energy we are projecting. Choose to project energies of love, perceiving people the way God perceives them. As you do, you help others remember their wholeness.

How Much Joy Can You Hold?

As humans we have a harder time staying in joy than we do in pain and struggle. Joy is a very high, clear vibration in which life flows effortlessly and gracefully. Pain is a slow, low vibration that attracts disharmony and upsets into our life. When we are in pain and struggle. We are cut off from our natural connection to the heavens and the light of Christ-energy. This energy source that sustains all life and from which all creation comes, is meant to flow to us freely, easily, and abundantly. It is our God-given *natural* state to be in the high vibration of joy, yet for must humans it is not the *familiar* state.

Let me explain what I mean by *natural* and *familiar.* "Natural" means what we have been created to experience effortlessly and spontaneously as our genuine selves. God created us to experience joy as our natural state. What is natural is enthusiasm. What is natural to you is laughing a lot. What is natural is feeling strong and secure. What is natural is a zest for life beyond anything most people over eight years old have felt for a long, long time.

"Familiar" means what has become commonplace and habitual because of how frequently we have experienced it in our lives. Pain and struggle have become the familiar life experience for most people. It is unfamiliar to be happy and joyful all the time, intentionally choosing to create more and more of what brings increased joy to others and ourselves.

Staying in a high vibration of joy and happiness, and creating a wonderful life is every person's opportunity and one of the primary purposes of the time in which we live. To achieve and maintain this high vibratory state, we must become aware of the patterns we continually recreate that put us in pain and struggle. As well as becoming aware of these patterns, we need to understand why we create them. For most people there is a belief that they add some value to our lives. Some of the most common beliefs that my clients have identified include:

- ❖ We believe our spiritual exaltation and advancement is directly connected to how much hardship we overcome in this life.
- ❖ We believe if life were easy and pain-free, we might get bored or have nothing to challenge us.
- ❖ We believe it keeps us humble.
- ❖ We believe that living in a constant state of joy and happiness is a facade and means we are not willing to deal with the realities of life.
- ❖ We are humans, and humans like drama.

I have also worked with many clients that honestly do not know what a life of joy and happiness is like. They have never experienced true happiness and unconditional love in their entire lives because of abusive parents, conditional support, and adult lives riddled with dysfunction. They are stuck in a pattern of upset and disharmony and keep unconsciously recreating this pattern because it is all that they have known. They are not even sure what it would feel like to be loved just for themselves, and to have a life free of pain and struggle. Some are afraid to introduce this into their lives for fear that if they have it, they may lose it, and that would be too difficult. They believe it is easier living with the pain and managing it, rather than knowing true joy and happiness and then losing it. As my clients learn new life skills and become aware of their creative powers, they realize they are unconsciously creating their current circumstances of hardship and struggle and they have the power to create a life of joy. They realize there is no risk, because they are the ones in charge of their life experiences and the results they are getting.

Examine your own beliefs. If you were told you could have a life completely free of pain and hardship, would you believe it were possible? What do you believe the struggles and hardships of your life offer you? Do you believe you could create those same benefits and claim those same blessings in a constant state of joy and happiness and prosperity? If you lived in a constant state of joy and happiness and prosperity, could you stay in a place of compassion and humility? Do you need adversity to keep you humble and submissive to God? As long as pain and struggle has a hidden value to you, you will need it in your life.

There will always be opposition in all things. That does not mean there has to be struggle in all things. The contrast with which we all live is meant to be a medium to distinguish the opposites. Without *dark*, we could not know *light*. Without *pain*, we could not know *joy*. Without *up*, we could not know *down*. Without *hate*, we could not know *love*. Opposites exist so that we can have a choice. It is because of the contrast that we are able to know what we want, by experiencing what we do not want. It is through contrast that these choices are possible and the function of our agency is constantly employed. You will always have the opportunity to dip into the pool of contrast to create what you don't want, so you can become more aware of what you do want.

I believe pain and struggle has been the primary medium for spiritual advancement for mankind. We have needed adversity and hardships to know our higher selves and awaken our god-like traits. I believe that in the new millennium we are free to graduate to a different experience of spiritual advancement. I believe we can choose spiritual advancement through the avenues of intention and desire. I believe that through our intentions to become our higher selves and become like Christ, we can create this. I believe that through desire we can create lives of joy and happiness and prosperity and at the same time choose to be a reverent, loving, compassionate, obedient, and humble people.

There will always be the contrast of pain and hardship available to us. The old belief has been, *I am learning and growing through adversity.* The new belief can be, *I am learning and growing through joy.* The question to ask yourself now is, *How much joy can you hold, and how long can you hold it?*

WE ARE ALL ONE

Every human being is subconsciously and energetically connected to every other human being on the planet. When we heal and progress spiritually, we benefit the entire human race. Human consciousness is interconnected, and when one person raises his or her level of spiritual consciousness, everyone else gets a piece of it.

An example is the first four-minute mile. When Roger Bannister ran the mile in less than four minutes, he broke an energy ceiling in our consciousness. Until someone ran a mile in less than four minutes, most people believed it was not possible. This created a limitation in our consciousness that made it harder to achieve this feat. However, when this feat was achieved, everyone claimed to have believed that it could be done. This lifted the energy ceiling we had collectively created as a human race. In a very short time after the first four-minute mile, many other individuals also ran the four-minute mile because we believed it was possible.

As you continue to choose to become more spiritually enlightened and advanced, you make it easier for others to do the same. We are literally serving the entire human race when we are in a vibration of compassion and embody the Christ-like qualities of unconditional love and allowing.

When you choose to heal the negative beliefs and emotions that are keeping you stuck and clear generational patterns from your DNA, everyone in your family benefits from this choice. I have witnessed many clients' family members come into more harmony and union when only one person in the family came in to do sessions with me. When we clear our inherited emotional disharmonies from our DNA, it is as if we genetically came from this clearer state. Our generations are cleared from the same patterns we are clearing. We offer a great service to our ancestors and posterity as we reclaim our spiritual wholeness. Our ancestors are freer to claim their wholeness and our posterity is born with more of their wholeness intact.

⁓

Amanda had not heard from her adult son in two years. He had separated from his family bitter and angry and requested that he be left alone until he contacted them. She knew he still lived in the same state but had no information about his location. There was a pattern in their family of people leaving. Those that left carried a deeper belief that they could not be loved for just themselves. They believed there were conditions and expectations they had to live up to in order to be acceptable and loved. They left because they could no longer play out the roles that had been imposed on them.

Amanda recognized this pattern and admitted that her first husband (her son's father) had been very conditional and authoritarian to the children. She chose to be powerless to his dysfunctional behaviors and never intervened on her children's behalf. Even though his mother was no longer married to his father, her son still carried the wounds of his childhood and the perception that his mother did not care about him either.

We did a process in behalf of her son, which is called a "proxy clearing." Because energy is free form, it can be cleared for others by setting an intention and focusing on the individual for whom you are proxying. I had Amanda visualize her son in his wounded state. She imagined him standing in the light with her and Christ. I told her to imagine herself as a being of white light and to ask her son if he would like to be assisted. She felt he did. At this point I instructed her to imagine herself free of her physical body and become a being of light that could be one with him and his energy. At that point we started the clearing process as if he were the one sitting in the chair in the session with me.

As Amanda continued to come in for herself, we spent a portion of each session doing a proxy clearing on behalf of her son. Many of the beliefs, emotions, and patterns we were clearing for him were appropriate for her to clear as well since there is a generational theme in everyone's negative energy.

Along with the proxy clearings we were doing in her sessions, I suggested she imagine her son in a daily meditation. In this meditation she was to imagine him in a place of white light with Christ where she was to send him the energy of unconditional love and allowing. To telepathically send to his subconscious mind the message that there were no longer any conditions imposed on him to be loved and accepted as an important member of the family. That he was free to be himself and she would love him free of any expectations. She also sent the message that she loved him and wanted to hear from him.

At the time she concluded her sessions with me she had still not heard from her son and still did not know where he was living. About a year later I ran into Amanda at a restaurant. We were able to talk privately, so I asked her how she was doing and if she had heard from her son. With tears in her eyes, she shared with me that just a few months earlier, he had called her at home and wanted to see her. And he had recently moved back in with her for a short period. She knew that she had helped this transition to occur through her proxy clearings and meditations with him. She was grateful for the time with him home again where she could now show up for him as a loving, supportive mother.

As Amanda had come to learn, it is never too late to give your children the emotional and spiritual support they deserve. No matter the age of your children—whether small, teenage, or adult—if they have not heard the messages that fill their emotional needs, they will be looking for someone in their life to fill them. As their parent you have the stewardship to offer this to the children that came into your family. If you have neglected this sacred contract, then you will be held accountable. It is never too late to tell your children in spoken and unspoken communication the messages they are longing to hear. These messages include:

❖ We are glad you are in our family.
❖ There is nothing you have to do to be loved.
❖ You are important to us.
❖ Your needs and desires are important.
❖ You are loved for just being you.
❖ You are important, and you have a special purpose in life.
❖ You are a child of God, and he loves you.
❖ I love to hold you and nurture you.
❖ The family is more complete because you are in it.

Ask angels to orchestrate opportunities every day for you to affirm your children. Moments will occur when you will be filled with loving energy and the words that will flow easily to affirm their great worth. Even if your children are adults, they will still love to hear these messages from you. Ask angels to orchestrate moments in your phone calls and interactions where it will happen naturally. If you have little or no contact with your children, choose to send these messages to their subconscious minds and the energy of your love to surround them.

Because we are all one big network of energy, we can influence others' healing and the entire human race waking up to our Christ-consciousness. It will be like the hundredth monkey syndrome. When a certain number of us have awakened, then the entire human race will be shifted into higher states of consciousness naturally and effortlessly. One day your family and your neighbors will just wake up as highly evolved spiritual beings and think they have always been that way!

EVERYONE IS PSYCHIC

Webster's Dictionary defines the word "psychic" as someone who communicates with spirit. The *American Heritage Dictionary* defines it as extraordinary, extrasensory, and nonphysical mental processes.

According to the above definitions, everyone is psychic because everyone has spiritual gifts and capacities he or she is meant to be using more intimately to guide and direct his or her life. We have become conditioned to using our physical senses and logical thinking minds as the compass of our lives. By fine-tuning our spiritual senses, we will be able to choose more effortlessly, with fewer and fewer detours, the direction our lives could be taking.

Spiritual gifts include intuition, discernment, precognition, spiritual empathy, visionary, working of miracles, powers of healing, and powers to be healed.

Spiritual Gifts	My Definition
Intuition	A clear knowledge or insight of what is right for you, free of any logical or rational processes.

Discernment:	A capacity to be sensitive to the less obvious and to perceive the obscure or concealed.
Precognition:	The knowledge of something in advance of its occurrence knowing something is going to happen before it does, knowing what someone is going to say before they say it.
Spiritual Empathy	Knowing the condition of someone's life and welfare without having to ask.
Visionary Spiritual	Sight, including prophecy and revelation for one's life. Also includes seeing the finer energy around us like colors and energy fields.
Working of Miracles	Communicating with the Spirit to ask the Spirit to bless lives and initiate powerful events that manifest in the physical realm.
Powers of Healing	Asking the Spirit to heal a physical, emotional or mental disharmony on behalf of some-

one who wants to be healed.

Powers to be Healed   Having the faith to be the recipient of healing powers.

⌒

Laura was an angel and she had forgotten. I met her when I went to her for a massage. She asked me what I did and I told her that I was a Spiritual Therapist and that I used a tool to help people clear the energies and beliefs that interfere with fulfilling their spiritual purpose easily and gracefully. She shared with me that she felt she had spiritual gifts that she wanted to use but didn't know how. I gave her my card and before we parted that day I felt strongly impressed to share a message with her. I told her that she was an angel and was meant to make a difference in many people's lives.

I asked her if she spent a lot of time doing things for others, but felt worn out and unappreciated. She said she did. I have found that people who have angelic energy can get stuck in patterns of helping others whose lives are in a lot of crisis who are not responsive to change. These angelic beings end up giving a lot of time and energy to these people although nothing ever gets better. They know they are meant to make a difference, yet their deeper feelings of worthlessness set them up to attract individuals who use them and expect a lot from them without giving anything in return.

Laura called me to set up an appointment a short while after our meeting. She saw me for several sessions, and in that time she cleared many of her limiting and self-defeating subconscious beliefs. She started to actualize her spiritual gifts and use them to bless others' lives in her work and personal relationships. She used her empathic skills to know how her clients were feeling and accessed a lot of insight on her clients' behalf without asking a lot of questions. She became more aware of her powers of healing through her skills as a massage therapist. Laura cleared the belief that she had to help others to feel good about herself. She successfully changed that belief to, *I am worthwhile and lovable and I am choosing to help others feel better and get well.*

As a result, Laura changed her pattern of attracting people who did not benefit from her gifts and skills, to attracting like-minded people who achieved great results from their sessions with her and returned for more. In her personal life, she had more time for herself and was now free to create relationships wherein she experienced more harmony and mutual respect. She used her powers of intuition more as things started to change in her life. She moved to a new city, was led to a better place to work, increased her income, and met a man that she created a healthy, loving relationship with.

Throughout this period of change, Laura questioned and scrutinized the impressions and inspirations she was receiving. In the early stages she easily doubted and was concerned it all just might be a crazy idea that would not work out. With encouragement, she increasingly trusted more and more without having to know the outcome. She learned to identify the feelings within her that are given to each of us as signals to know what is right for our lives. When I know something is right, I have a distinct feeling in my chest area. It almost feels like a burning in my heart.

⁓

Intuition is a feeling and a mental clarity that cannot be rationalized. I encourage my clients to be wise in who they choose to share their inspirations with. If shared with a "doubting Thomas" they will invite skepticism, which will add to any of their own doubts.

By trusting our intuition, we are brought the physical evidence of our making the right choice soon after the decision. As we continue this cycle of allowing the inspirations to come, acting on it, followed by positive results, our intuition will continue to build and grow and become very strong and natural. It will become the primary way of knowing what choices to make and what direction to move in life.

Intuition and all other spiritual gifts are powers given to us by God that are to be trusted and acted upon. By not using them, they become dormant and absent to us. You must ask God to help you know what your spiritual gifts are and how to implement them into your daily experience. All spiritual gifts are available to everyone. If there are any gifts you would like to have, just ask that your spirit be endowed with the gift and the Holy Spirit will bestow it upon you. Then use it to make a positive difference in your life and the lives of others.

CHAPTER 25

Unconditional Love Is the Most Powerful Force in the Universe

Unconditional love, the most powerful force in the Universe, is available to everyone. Love is an energy, a power, and a force. Someday scientists may be able to explain the physics of love and give scientific evidence of its existence. Until then we can have faith that this power exists on our behalf and call upon it to bless our lives. I believe the origin of this love is God the Father and Mother and their Son, Jesus Christ.

How does it benefit our lives to incorporate this energy? How do we practically implement the forces of unconditional love into our daily experiences to improve the quality of our lives? I prayerfully asked these questions. These are the answers God shared with me.

He told me to first consider the word *unconditional*. It means unlimited, unrestricted, unqualified, absolute, complete, with no conditions attached. These are the characteristics of God and Christ. This force in the Universe is unrestricted, it is everywhere, is unlimited in nature, absolute, and complete with no conditions attached to receiving it. The energy of unconditional love is in the makeup of everything. It is the eternal matter that is the origin of all creation. It is the highest and purest vibration available to us.

We are given experiences daily that allow us to make choices that support us in being in the energy of unconditional love. To be in a state of compassion and a state of allowing keeps us in the energy of unconditional love. When we are in the energy of unconditional love, we are in a powerful position to bless and grace the lives of others.

The day that I asked God the question of how to implement and use this energy in my life, I had the following experience. I was standing in the checkout line of a craft store waiting my turn. The Holy Spirit told me to look at the people around me, the people in line, and the store clerk. I was told that each of these people would be blessed if I asked that the energy of unconditional love be given to them in that moment. I was told that if I would exercise this practice of silently asking for this blessing for others while I was in their presence, it would be returned to me multiplied, and I would secretly have the capacity to change others' lives as well as my own.

We are admonished to serve others in secret. I remember reading several years ago in Marianne Williamson's book, *A Return to Love,* that those who have awakened to their god-self within are God's miracle workers. She said, "To become a miracle worker means to take part in a spiritual underground that's revitalizing the world, participating in a revolution of the world's values at the deepest possible level. That doesn't mean you announce this to anyone. A member of the French underground didn't walk up to a German officer occupying Paris and say 'Hi, I'm Jacques. French Resistance." Similarly, you don't tell people who would have no idea what you're talking about, 'I'm changed. I'm working for God now. He sent me to heal things. The world is about to shift big time.' Miracle workers learn to keep their own counsel. Something that's important to know about spiritual wisdom is that when spoken at the wrong time, in the wrong place, or to the wrong person, the one who speaks sounds more like a fool than a wise one."[15]

When we secretly call upon the Heavens to bless others' lives, our service is not meant to be known to them. It would have been very strange to the people in the craft store if I had said, "All of you look like you could use a little unconditional love energy, so I called upon the Spirit in your behalf and it has been given to you." And yet spoken in secret it is a great service of which each of us can be more aware, and give freely without any physical effort or time on our part.

If you believe that what we give out returns to us multiplied, then if everyone reading this book practiced this service at least once a day, we would call forth a powerful healing energy into our physical realm in a profound manner. I encourage you to do this. Make it a practice that becomes as common as brushing your teeth every day.

The love that emanates to us from God is the most powerful force in the Universe. It is abundant and free for the asking. Remember that it is unconditional, so when you feel the most unworthy of it, that is just your perception and probably when you could use it the most. God is unconditional in his offering; choose to be unconditional to yourself in your asking and receiving. God loves you and wants you to have the experience of feeling sustained by this energy.

---

[15] Marianne Williamson. *A Return to Love*. New York, NY: Harper Perennial. 1992. pg. 68.

Have you ever had the experience of talking to someone or listening to music and being present in a particular environment and you felt all warm and fuzzy inside? As if someone were hugging you on the inside? You did not want this experience to end, because you did not want the feeling to leave. This is what it feels like to be held in the energy of unconditional love. God wants to share it with everyone and he will if we just ask. He has told us, "Ask and ye shall receive." If I am asking for myself, I say, *Thank you, God, for encircling me in the arms of your love.* I imagine I am surrounded in a bubble of white light and angels are anointing me. I can lie in my bed in the morning and feel enclosed by a very warm and tender energy that is holding me. If I am asking for others I say, *Thank you, God, for flowing your love into the presence of this individual person or group of people.* Since this energy is unbounded, unrestricted, and unlimited, you can play with it in a big way to affect a lot of people at once.

The next time you are at a very large event, like a play, concert, or sporting event, ask for this energy to flow to everyone in attendance and for the Heavens to part and angels to come down and minister to all present. Do you get the picture? Do you realize the powers of Heaven you have at your disposal? Do you realize that when you ask, you receive, and what you have asked for is manifest, and in that asking you are changing the world?

CHAPTER 26

Angels Are Among Us

Want to change your world? There is nothing to it when you use the powers of your imagination and the powers of Heaven to assist you. When Henry Ford said, "anything you can imagine is possible" he was right.

We live in a time when Heaven and its powers are very close to us. The veil that was placed over us at birth is becoming very thin. We literally walk among angels—angels that are physical, and angels that are spiritual. I would like to focus on the spirit angels and their desire to serve us.

When you think of Heaven and its resources, imagine Heaven right here with us. Angels walk before us and by our side daily. They prepare the way for our day to go smoothly. They assist us in orchestrating the details of our lives so we don't have to. They assist us by creating in spirit that for which we have asked, so that we can manifest it in the physical realm effortlessly. They anoint us and help us heal while we are sleeping. Angels are our guardians and stewards. The purpose of their creation is to serve humanity. They want to adorn us with support, direction, protection, and assistance. There are multitudes of angels and heavenly hosts to call upon, and yet many people do not call upon them for a variety of reasons.

We have been taught to pray to God and to ask him to help us. If we start asking angels for help, where does that put God in our lives? It is my belief and practice that I pray to my Father in Heaven in the name of Jesus Christ. I believe that God has an entire universe full of spirit beings directed by the Holy Spirit to use for our benefit. They assist and serve God by helping us. We each have spiritual agreements and callings; angels have accepted the calling to serve humanity. It is up to us to ask them to help us.

Everyone has legions of spirit assistance at their disposal, yet most people doubt that it can be as simple as asking for it and allowing it to show up in their lives. Instead of asking for what they want and believing they can have it, most people instead respond to the conditions of their life. Most people spend much of their time observing their life and what they don't like about it, and observing others' lives, making judgments about them. Most people are not being deliberate about what they want, and setting an intention that it will come forth.

Many people are intimidated and think it is silly to talk to angels. Most people do not know how to access these resources in their day-to-day life experiences. We seem to believe that we can only ask for spiritual intervention and assistance with the big, important, or challenging aspects of our lives. But God wants us to invoke our spiritual resources to help us accomplish mundane as well as inspired tasks. When we ask for the intervention of the Heavens in all aspects of our lives, we will experience more and more of our lives unfolding to a higher will and not just our will alone.

Do you need to know who the angels are and call them by name? No, that is not necessary. Some people do; I don't. Their identity to me is a vibration rather then an earthly name. They speak the language of spirit, which is a language of feeling. I do not see them, yet I know they are with me all the time because I feel them. I make so many requests that I am sure I have received help from hundreds of angels—more than I can keep track of.

Janice was entering her junior year in college. Having an intense history of sexual abuse in her child-hood, she had been afraid of men her entire life. She experienced great success in her sessions: clearing her very wounded inner-child, meeting her unmet needs, creating new beliefs, and coming into more and more of her adult energy. She had been on very few dates in her life because every time she did date, her wounded inner-child would get triggered into fear, and her body would create stomachaches and headaches that would force her to end the date early, so she could go home and go to bed.

After several sessions she told me she was ready to experience meeting and dating more guys. She decided she wanted to date a lot of different guys with the possibility of meeting the man she would want to marry within the school year.

She wrote this down and was specific in saying she wanted at least three dates a month, and she wanted them to be with guys that were safe, respectful, easy to have fun with, and easy to talk to. I told her to imagine her Dating Angels and ask them to scan the campus to find the guys, and orchestrate the dates showing up easily for her.

The first three months of school went by and she was averaging one to two dates a week—more than the three a month for which she had asked. She was meeting a lot of nice guys that were fun and easy to be with. In the third month of school she was reunited with a man she had met the year before but had never dated. She started to date him, and they fell in love. They were engaged before the school year ended and married the next summer. Throughout the course of these events, fears would surface for Janice and she would resort to old thought and behavior patterns of sabotage. We continued to clear old energies from her childhood, and she continued to create new beliefs and life skills that allowed her to marry a man she dearly loves. To this day she acknowledges her Dating Angels as being instrumental in bringing them together.

We can also ask God in our prayers for angels to help others. We can ask for angels to guide and protect our children, spouses, and other loved ones. When I know of tragedies happening in the world, I ask that as many angels as necessary go to minister unto those in pain. We can ask for angels to minister to those who are sick and afflicted. We can ask to have angels go with us to friends' and families' houses to brighten the space and add the feelings of fun, unconditional love and acceptance to all those who will be present. Whenever I go into a public space or someone else's home, I ask for angels to go before me to clear any dark or disharmonious energies, and to fill the space with light.

When I notice negative energy around people or in the place where I am, I ask for angels to come and create a vortex of light to remove the negative energy and recycle it into light energy. Many of my clients unconsciously take on heavy, negative energy to help others feel better or to clear out disharmonies in the places they've been during the day. They feel tired a lot and have a hard time feeling positive. Many of the negative emotions they are feeling are not even their own. I teach them how to become aware of energies outside of themselves and how to ask for spiritual assistance to clear it so they are not part of the process of channeling it.

When my oldest daughter was in the seventh grade, she started coming home from school with severe headaches and was very tired. She felt overwhelmed a lot of the time and seemed overly worried for her young age. If she watched the news, she would frequently have horrific dreams that the world was at war, and it was up to her to save the children by facilitating world peace. I expressed to God, *Thank you for impressing upon my mind what I need to know about Jennifer to eliminate the stress she is feeling to her body and spirit.*

At the time I was studying Reiki and reading *Quantum Healing* by Deepak Chopra. The thoughts started to form that at school Jenny was taking on the negative emotion others were emitting as a service to help them feel better. One of her spiritual purposes is to awaken the light in others and to help them feel better about themselves. Her spirit was anxious to be active in this role, and yet she was not involved consciously with her spirit to direct it. As a result she was suffering unnecessarily. I taught her how to protect herself and call upon the powers of heaven to help people clear negative emotions without any detriment to her.

If you sense this is happening to you, ask to be surrounded by white and gold light. Ask the Holy Spirit to send angels to the place you are going or to the place you are, to clear any negative energies and to surround everyone present with white and gold light. You do not need to take on the negative energies of others. Let spirit do it for you.

As we remember to ask our spirit friends and helpers to grace our lives with their powers, we will not only be aided by our lives running more smoothly, we will also be aided in our healing and in the reclaiming of our wholeness. Angels work with our souls, in conjunction with Christ energy, to help us raise our vibration and state of consciousness. They remind us of truth and facilitate the awakening of the truth that lies within each of our cells when we are ready to integrate it into our daily lives. As I walk with my angels and friends of light, I know that I am never alone. I know that I am always aided, and that there is help and guidance all around me. I now live in a state of gratitude in which I experience miracles occurring regularly.

A prayer I frequently offer before I fall asleep at night is:

Thank you, God, for sending healing angels to minister over me tonight. To assist me in clearing, healing, and awakening on all levels while I am sleeping. I am experiencing my real self more clearly, presently, and focused in my day-to-day life. I ask for this in the name of Jesus Christ, amen.

HOW TO PETITION YOUR ANGELS

Knowing how to call upon the powers of heaven will dramatically change your life. Imagine that you have a whole crew of angels around you to assist you with whatever request you make of them. The only criterion is that your requests cannot be hurtful to another. Angels and other beings of light will only assist and orchestrate on our behalf when we are choosing things of the light.

Start by deciding what you want in your life. An easy writing process to help you become clearer in knowing what you want is to identify first what you don't want. Take a piece of paper and on one side list, "What I Don't Want." On the other side list, "What I Do Want." Ask yourself the question, *If my life were ideal, what would it look like?*

I tell my clients that if God were to come to you and say, "George, you can have your life be any way you want it to be. Tell me how you want it to be, and I'll help you create it." What would you tell God? I counsel the person to only imagine what they can honestly believe is possible for them. If they do not believe it could happen easily, they will doubt. Doubt energy is a heavy energy that disconnects us from source energy. This creates resistance on our part, which interferes with allowing what we have asked for to manifest easily.

In this process write the ideal you really believe could happen. List desires that include your relationships, career, body, mind, state of abundance, home, transportation, and spiritual and family life. Or take one of these areas and list what you want in detail. Remember, the more specifically you ask for what you want, the more specifically you will receive it.

Deciding what you want is the first step in setting into motion the creation of what you want. The second step that allows it to come effortlessly into your life is to play a game I call, "Ask Your Angels."

Take your list, all or part, and write at the top, "Thank you for orchestrating the details for the following desires to come into my life effortlessly and joyfully." Close your eyes and imagine a spiritual crew receiving your requests and going to work to make them happen for you. Your job now is to want it, believe it, allow it, and appreciate it. It will happen.

Unfortunately, it is common that in the beginning of a client's experience with this process, they become clear on what they want, set it into motion by asking for it, and then create resistance. Resistance is created by doubting it, making statements that counter it happening, continually looking for it to happen, feeling suspicious that it won't, and trying to figure out how to make it happen.

Let's say you want a new white car. You write down your intention: "Thank you for bringing a new car into my life. I want it to be white, to be in this price range, and I want it to be this kind of car. I want one that will require low maintenance, will run well, and be a joy to drive." After you write this down and release it to the Universe, you find yourself talking to a friend and you tell them you hope to get a new white car. But because you are not sure you are going to get it, you speak words of doubt, which create a vibration that blocks the car from showing up. You might say things like "I'm going to get a new car, but I just can't find one that is in my price range." "I want a new car but the color and model I want is pretty scarce."

In your mind you think you have to figure out where the car is going to come from, and that you have to get busy to make it happen. You don't give the Universe the chance to orchestrate the details and flow the information and events into your life because you're too focused on trying to figure it out yourself. Once you have offered your intention and asked for a new white car, release it to the Universe by asking your angels for assistance and allow it to show up. Events, ideas, and inspired action will synchronistically come to you, and you will soon have your new white car. Remember, when you want it and don't resist it, it comes every single time without exception.

When you start playing this game of asking your angels to assist you, all kinds of things will open up to you. As I look back on my experience of asking my angels, in the beginning I asked for very few things. Now I ask for their help with everything. I realized that the Universe has enormous resources to help me. I started noticing many of the things I was asking for were happening without my needing to take any action at all. My job is to identify what I want, to ask for it, allow it, and to say thank-you when it comes.

I ask for assistance with everything in my life. Each day I awake imagining my spiritual crew ready and anxious to honor me and help me with my requests. I have a section in my day planner I call, "Ask My Angels." Each morning I have a meeting with them and write down the things on which I would like them to work. Here is a typical day's request:

❖ Thank you for flowing to me the ideas of what to buy at the grocery store today to make easy, delicious, healthy meals this week.

❖ Please orchestrate my day so I am involved and participating in those activities that serve my highest good.

❖ Please find me a rental car at a low rate in Hawaii for our July trip.

❖ I want my clients to refer my services to people who will be blessed and whose lives will be better from seeing me.

❖ Orchestrate a tennis match for me tomorrow, early morning or afternoon.

❖ Thank you for helping my daughter know what to do in her current situation, and to be fueled with love and honor for herself.

❖ Thank you for assisting my son and me in having a playful, trusting relationship.

❖ When we go to Palm Springs over spring break, I want fabulous weather and a safe and fun car ride down there. I want to play tennis three to four times and to play golf with our entire family.

❖ Thank you for finding us tickets to Disneyland at a discount.

I look at the list above, and everything I asked for happened. When I asked for the discounted tickets to Disneyland, I had no idea where these would come from. I was not aware of a place to buy them. Within two days of asking, I told a friend we were going to Disneyland and she said, "Would you like me to get you discounted tickets? My husband can get them through his work!" When synchronicity like this happens (which is all the time in my life), I am no longer surprised. I am very pleased, excited, and appreciative. In my mind, I think of my angel friends, chuckle, and tell them thanks. I notice myself thinking a lot, *You guys crack me up! Thanks for making it so fun!*

When someone in our family has lost or misplaced something, I'll ask them, "Have you asked your angels to find it for you?" Whenever this happens to me, I let go of trying to find the item myself and turn it over to my angels by saying, "Thank you for finding such and such." I know I will come across it or have the idea of where to look come into my mind momentarily. It always does, and I always find it.

While driving in the car one day with my teenage daughter, Anne turned to me and asked, "Do you know why all the lights are turning green for us?"

I said, "No, why?"

She smiled, "I have green-light angels. They go ahead of us to all the lights we are coming to and make sure they are green by the time we get there."

From that point on, every time we went through the intersection we would celebrate and yell thank-you to Anne's green-light angels. If you go anywhere with Anne you will hit at least 90 percent of the lights green and frequently 100 percent of them.

I know the key in allowing the success we experience with spiritual assistance in our family is our faith. Faith, free of any doubt, is necessary to allow the stream of heavenly assistance to flow openly. Having faith is as simple as knowing we are deeply loved and important to the Heavens. They want to help us; they only see us with loving eyes. They applaud our efforts here on earth and commend us for our being here.

I love this process because it makes life so fun. I know that I can have anything I want. In my prayers I ask to be in harmony with God's will, and that I will only ask for that which is for my highest good. I know that God wants to bless us with all the good he has created. We each have our own room in Heaven filled with everything we could ever want in abundance, just waiting to be given to us. It is okay to have a grace-filled, easy life. You only need to keep the struggle and hardships if you still believe you need them to grow, to learn, and to stay in humility and service to God. Recently I heard two neighbors chatting about the purpose of hard times. One said to the other, "I told my daughter that I believe I learn and grow the most when things are really, really hard." As you wish!

I know it is possible to live a life free of mistakes, problems, disease, strain, and stress. We are unlimited creative beings. Every day you can make more and more decisions about what you want. Notice what you do not want; own it as your creation and ask yourself, *What do I want to create instead?* Have fun with this by playing with it. Keep noticing more and more what you do want.

I know we have within each of us the capacity to create lives of fulfillment—free from mistakes, problems, and illness. As we choose to acclimate to higher states of consciousness and a state of wholeness, our lives will be characterized by complete alertness and spontaneous use of our full potential. We are meant to take command over our destiny, with the organizing power to accomplish any worthy goal without strain.

God wants us to incorporate the resources he has provided for us. Stop thinking your only relationships are in the physical realm. Call upon those in the spirit realm and let them do for you what you no longer have to do for yourself. Activate these beliefs in every cell of your body by offering the following prayer:

I am grateful for my life of bliss and joy. All things come to me easily. I now choose to learn and grow through joyous experiences. I am calling upon the powers of Heaven to assist me daily. I am coming to know the Universe as my home and all the beings of light that reside within it as my family. I am ready to come home to my truth. Thank you, God, that I am remembering who I am and the purpose for which I have come in this physical creation. I am obedient and I am free. I am serving thee willingly and lovingly. I know thou loves me and will continue to assist me in creating a quality of bliss and wholeness that pervades my existence. Thank you. Thank you. Thank you. In the name of Jesus Christ, amen.

I have offered you my experience of how I more fully draw upon the powers of Heaven. Prayerfully seek to understand how to use the spiritual powers that are available to you. There is spiritual help for you if you ask for it. Come to know how to petition the assistance of angels in a manner that is appropriate with your spiritual beliefs.

THE POWER OF SYNCHRONICITY

Synchronicity is defined as odd or unusual events that happen at unexpected times. These events seem strangely to coordinate to create desired outcomes. Synchronicity follows the law of least effort. The details of life easily and often fall into place with unpredictable timing.

When we call upon the powers of Heaven to assist us by taking care of the details of our life, synchronicity should be expected. Our role is to desire and to ask for what we want. Our world of contrast, or opposites, exists so we can have a variety of choices. Desire for what we want is born out of the contrast. It is as if we are moving along the hall of life and there are a lot of doors to open. Each door represents a different experience. As we move through the hall of life, we are meant to open the doors and enter into different experiences. We are meant to notice the experiences we don't want, and then to open more doors of the experiences we do want.

Synchronicity is the Holy Spirit's way of letting us know we are moving into or choosing experiences that are in harmony with our core desires. Synchronicity operates effortlessly. The doors that are right for us to move through open effortlessly. The first door leads to more doors that we can open, and the details come together beautifully and in perfect time. When a situation or choice is not in our highest good, synchronicity is nonexistent, and the doors are hard to open. The Holy Spirit is letting us know that if we push against a situation and it pushes back, it is not right for us, or the timing is not correct.

Notice what you are trying to force in your life. Possibly, you have convinced yourself that what you are trying to make happen is supposed to happen. It is amazing how many people, because of their ego's needs, would rather be right than happy. Let go of being right, and choose to open doors to experiences that offer you happiness. Many people are stuck in patterns of struggle that make the past, present, and future seem like they are all the same, and that life will never get any better. They just keep going through the same door, living through the same experiences in a state of mediocrity because it is familiar to them.

By asking God and his angels to assist you in creating a new life, you will have faster and better results if you let go of the details and let heavenly powers take care of them. When we want a change for the better to occur in our lives, it may be necessary to let go of some of our current situations to create a space for new ones to show up.

Maureen was a single woman, bored with her job. Her relationships were very one-way, where she did most of the giving. She felt lonely and was ready for a close relationship with a man. As she cleared her deeper beliefs, emotions, and patterns that were keeping her stuck in her life of mediocrity and loneliness, the desires of her real self started to manifest.

She wanted a job where she could travel and have more money. She wanted relationships that were balanced and harmonious where both parties invested their energies. She wanted to meet a man who wanted to create a loving, playful, respectful, trusting, and spiritual relationship with her.

Her first step was to have a desire for a new life. As she let this desire grow within her, she was able to be more specific in her intentions. She then asked the Universe to work to bring this into her life. Her job was to respond to any prompting and synchronistic events—to notice which doors opened effortlessly and to move through them, moving past the doors that were difficult to open.

The sequence of events that occurred very quickly in her life took her by surprise. The owner of her condominium decided to put it up for sale, which required her to move suddenly. Her employer decided to relocate and Maureen was not sure she wanted to follow. At first Maureen was nervous about letting go of these familiar conditions. She understood and trusted that to get the new life she asked for she needed to let go of some of the details of her old life. As soon as she emotionally and mentally let go of her situation, the new started to form. She received several new job offers, but probably the most significant event was that she met a delightful man who was all—and more of—what she had asked for. The last I knew, she was in a successful relationship with him

and was planning to move to his city to take a job she
had been offered.

⌐⌐⌐

Maureen experienced the power of synchronicity. As we
align our will with God's will, which is for us to be happy, and
then ask for what we want, the Universe goes to great effort to
flow what we want to us effortlessly and easily. Due to our con-
ditioning that we believe that we have to earn what we get, too
often we move past the doors that have already opened for us.
"Ask, and ye shall receive; knock, and it shall be opened unto
you."[16] All we have to do is ask, then knock. Knocking is
acknowledging the desire. As we desire what we have asked for,
we are in a high vibration that draws what we have asked for into
our lives synchronistically.

✹

---

[16] Doctrine & Covenants 4:7.

CHAPTER 29

You Are a Creator

If you believe turning your life over to God means not making any choices or decisions, then you are forgetting your accountability to function as a conscious human being. You may be using turning your life over to God as an excuse for not wanting to take responsibility for the drama and disharmony you are creating. You are also misunderstanding the Taoist concept of being in the flow. To "be in the flow" is to be in harmony with the Universe. We have been given creative powers and are meant to participate in an active relationship with the Universe and its processes. It requires conscious intention and skill to start partnering with God to co-create the life you want. If you desire this way of being, you need to take responsibility for being the creator of your life. It won't just happen by itself.

How many times in life have you been excited and encouraged about life getting better, and then let old energy patterns of fear and doubt overcome and start to defeat you?

As you become more awake and aware, you will realize that you always have the choice to continue the past pattern and be in your old energy, or to choose the new energy. By keeping your intention signal strong and clear, and never giving up and surrendering to the old energy, your dreams will come true.

When you notice you are in an old energy pattern, say to yourself, *I must have wanted to experience this again. I am forgiving myself for thinking I deserve this. I am choosing to live in the new energy of me. I am loved, supported and now learning and growing through joyous experiences. I am experiencing that what I want is good and I can have it easily and effortlessly.*

We live on a planet of free choice. God has endowed each of us with the agency to create and govern our own lives. We have each been born with the light of Christ in us. Everyone has been blessed with a guidance system that is directly connected to the Holy Spirit and Christ energy. We each have the capacity of knowing, truly *knowing* what is right for us.

I have worked with numerous individuals who believe they don't know what is right for them, or if they do, they don't expect it to happen or believe they can have it. They have developed patterns of thinking that others' needs and wants are first and ignoring their own. In most cases they are completely out of touch with their own needs, wants, and desires, because they are so conditioned to making sure others are happy. This behavior is typically a byproduct of their childhood experience with their parents. In most cases, as children, they sacrificed having their own needs met in lieu of their mother's needs being met. As a small child they believed that if they did not have any needs maybe Mom would be happier. They have deeply held beliefs like:

❖ Mom's needs are more important then mine. This translates in their adult life to, other's needs are more important than mine.

❖ My needs and desires don't matter.

❖ If I ask for it, I won't get it.

❖ It's okay if it doesn't happen because I really didn't want it anyway.

❖ I'm not important.

❖ I want others to know what I need without asking.

❖ I have to please others to be okay.

Someone with these deeper beliefs typically has a pattern of justifying, defending, and explaining themselves when they ask for what they want or when they share a decision they have made about their lives.

⁓

Every time I asked my client Stacey, "What do you want," she replied, "I don't know." She responded, "I don't know," dozens of times during her session. She was stuck in a state of "not knowing." She had been raised by a mother that was very depressed and unhappy. She discovered that as a small child she had abandoned her own needs and desires in the hope that trying to meet her mother's needs would help her feel happy. I asked her, "Did it work? Was your mother happier as a result of your efforts?" She said, "No!" I asked her, "Why are you still recreating this pattern for others in your life now? It didn't work then, why would it now?" She became more and more clear that every individual is in charge of creating his or her own happiness. We cannot do it for each other. We can only come together and add to the joy others are initiating for themselves.

As we worked at the subconscious level, clearing her inner-child fears and beliefs, Stacey began to experience the awakening of her own knowing. She recognized the habit she had of justifying, defending, and explaining herself when she shared with her husband what she knew was right for her. She wanted to go back to school and finish her degree. She only needed to complete less than a year of course work. She had left school when she had her first of two children because she did not want her children to make sacrifices for her as she had done for her mother. Now that her children were in grade school, she knew it would be manageable to go back to school. We wrote up scripts during her sessions and she practiced them. This was a new way of communicating for her, and she needed help with the words. I told her to start with a few simple decisions and get comfortable in stating what she wanted, free of the justifications. She started with things like, "I am going jogging and I'll be back in forty-five minutes. Thanks for watching the kids while I am gone." "No, I don't want to go to that movie. Is there another activity we could do that we both would enjoy?"

Stacey recognized that her belief in not being able to have what she wanted—and that if she did, others would not support her—attracted her husband and others to respond to her negatively. I asked her if she could imagine her husband being loving and supportive of her choices and decisions. At first this was hard because she had experienced him being resistive so many times in the past. I reminded her to observe less about what had happened in her life and imagine more of what she wanted. She took time to imagine her husband with a new script of loving, encouraging, and supporting her decisions. She practiced affirmations like, "I am saying what is right for me easily." "I am experiencing others are supportive of my choices."

She also asked her angels to orchestrate the details to make it possible for her to complete her schooling. As a result she attracted her husband and others to respond to her agreeably and supportively. When she shared with her husband that she knew it was right for her to go back to school, he was open to it and together they worked out a plan for this to happen. She experienced the power she has to create what she knew was right as her spirit was guiding her, and how to influence others showing up in support of her choices. She stopped saying, "I don't know," in her sessions and replaced it with, "I know what is right for me, and I am co-creating it with God and all the spiritual help he has provided for me."

If you have a pattern of justifying, defending, and explaining yourself, you still believe you are not good enough and you can't have what you want. You set yourself up to create disharmony in your desire because you kink up the energy of your desire manifesting easily by your deeper negative belief.

The next time you make a decision that is right for you and ask for what you want, believe you can have it. Let go of

justifying, explaining and defending your choice, and know that
God wants you to use your creative powers to bless your life.

This planet of free choice is continuing to move to her
heavenly celestial glory and to become a heaven on earth. As the
earth vibrates at a higher rate, we may find our bodies, emotions,
and mental states reacting in strange and different ways. The
exciting news is that as our creative powers are increasing, our
intentions, beliefs, and thoughts are manifesting almost
immediately.

Whether you believe it or not, you are the creator of
your reality. Start partnering with God to create a reality that
brings you joy. You'll find it easier and more fun than the painful
one you used to create.

CHAPTER 30

I AM DOING EVERYTHING YOU TEACH— WHY CAN'T I MANIFEST WHAT I WANT?

⁓

I teach the process of creation in a simple five-step process. Understanding this process, and practicing it to gain mastery, allows us to become master creators.

The first step is to know what you want. To have a desire.

Step two is to ask for what you want. Ask God. Ask the angels. Ask the Universe. You are asking a power greater than yourself to assist you in creating it.

Step three is to believe you can have it, to have faith, free of any doubt, that what you desire and have asked for is going to be manifest to you.

Step four is to let go and allow. To basically get out of your own way and allow spirit to be in charge of bringing your desire to you. The only job you have at this point is to follow through with any inspiration regarding your physical actions on behalf of your manifestation.

The fifth and last step is to express gratitude. Gratitude actually starts the cycle all over. It is the completion and the beginning of the creation process. Gratitude energy initiates more things manifesting in your life for which you feel gratitude. The creation process is one eternal round.

When practiced with humility it can only bring us more of what we want.

I am frequently asked the question "How come I am having such a hard time manifesting what I want? I have been practicing new beliefs and affirmations, I am following the steps, and it is still not happening!"

I teach the following technique to help people become clearer on why their desires are not showing up.

First, take your desire. Let's use the example of wanting a new car. Let's say you really want a car that is reliable, fun to drive, good looking, and reasonably priced. Rate your desire for a new car on a scale from 0-10, 10 being the strongest, 0 being the weakest.

For most people what they really want is a 10. So, in this case your desire for a new car is a 10.

Second, examine your belief. Do you believe that you deserve a new car? That you can have what you have asked for? That it will show up easily and effortlessly? That it will be as good or even better than what you have asked for?

Now rate your belief using the same 0-10 scale. Is your belief that you can have and receive what you want as strong as your desire? In the case of wanting a new car, let's pretend that your desire for one is a 10, yet your belief that you can and will have one is a 3.

This energy set up will keep you from attracting what you want! When there is a discrepancy between the energy of your desire and the energy of your belief you cannot attract into your life what you want.

When your desire is a 10 and your belief is a 10, you come into vibrational harmony with what you want and it shows up for you.

The next time you are frustrated because you are not manifesting what you want, rate your desire and your belief. How do they match up? Most people will shrink their desire rather than energize their belief and therefore settle for less. Instead of reducing your desire(s), energize your belief(s). If you reduce your desire and settle for less, you will feel disappointed and more convinced that you cannot have what you want. Energize your belief up to a 10 to match your desire with a process like an energy circle. (See the Appendix of Self-Help Processes for energy circle instructions.)

As you increase your belief(s) to match your desire(s), you will be amazed at how fast and flawlessly your desires manifest for you.

Another interference in manifesting what you want comes when you are emotionally attached to your desire. When you "need" what you have asked for and you are really fearful that it might not be manifest, you mess up the flow of it coming to you.

A method to help you let go of the fear is to imagine not getting what you have asked for. In your mind, imagine not getting what you want. It just doesn't happen. How do you feel? Ask yourself, *What is the worst thing that could happen if I don't get what I want?*

By asking yourself this question and being very honest with yourself with the answer, you realize that there is really nothing to be afraid of. You balance the energy by allowing yourself to imagine and feel your fear. This diffuses it and allows you to stay in a neutral place, which allows what you have asked for to show up.

Finally, if you are still not getting what you want, consider the possibility that your timing is off—it is just not the right time, or it is not in your highest and greatest good to receive it.

As you continue to play with these steps, make sure you are having fun. If you get serious and stressed with the steps, you will create all kinds of interference. Keep it light and free. We really do not "need" anything. Once we fully realize this, we let go and that is when the miracles really start to fly into our lives.

$\mathcal{E}$NERGIZING YOUR BELIEFS TO MANIFEST MORE OF WHAT YOU WANT

In the last chapter I introduced the rating system of rating your desires and your beliefs. For a quick review, when we have a desire and it is strong, let's say a 10 on a 0-10 scale, and your belief that it can happen is weaker than your desire, let's say a 4, you will have a kink in the energy and what you desire will not manifest for you easily.

Most people will lessen their desires and live in mediocrity because they are not aware that they really do have the power to realize their desires as the creators of their lives. In order to manifest our desires and create wonderful, joy-filled, rewarding lives, let's practice energizing our beliefs so they have the same energy of our desires, because when our desires are a 10 and our beliefs are a 10, the Law of Attraction delivers our desires to us. It's guaranteed.

Carol's Top Ten Belief Energizers:
1. Reduce the negativity that is keeping your belief small with a good old-fashioned RET session.
2. Ask your angels. When we think it all depends on us, we easily doubt. Know that you have a universal crew

at your disposal waiting to be employed. If you are not asking your staff of angels and beings of light to help you, they go unemployed. Get yourself out of the way and ask your angels to manifest your desires and you will be amazed at how magically your life falls into place. If there is anything you are to "do" in the process, you will receive inspiration to do it.

3. Play the "Act As If" game. Act as if you already have what you want and notice how good it feels. Tell your Creator "thank you" for how wonderful it is to be in your new experience.

4. Play the "Something Exciting Is About To Happen To Me" game. Dr. Joseph Bennette introduced me to this clever game. Just keep saying and thinking, *Something exciting is going to happen to me, I just know it! I can't wait to see what it is, and where it is going to show up.* Feel the goose-bumps on your arms and the tingling in your stomach. Remember when you were little and you were about to leave on a great vacation? The night before you could hardly get to sleep, but you knew when you did, suddenly it would be morning and you would wake up and get to go. Bring that feeling back to life and you will be amazed at what shows up for you.

5. Practice energy circles. Draw an imaginary circle on the ground in front of you and speak your desires into the circle. Build the energy of excitement as you speak, feeding your own belief that what you are asking for can really happen. Step into the circle and wash yourself

in the energy, then blow it out into the Universe to get the creation going. (See the Appendix of Self-Help Processes at the back of the book for more on energy circles.)

6. Go on a creation walk or run. While walking or running, pretend you are in your energy circle and it is moving along with you. Speak what you want as you take each step, pumping up the energy while you move. Occasionally throw your arms into the air shouting "Yes, thank you, Universe, for bringing all this to me!"

7. Stop talking about what you don't want and talk more about what you do want—with enthusiasm. Eliminate any reference to not having what you want in your day-to-day language and conversations.

8. Imagine more and observe less. As humans we tend to notice too often the current circumstances of our lives and then feel a lot of emotion about what we don't like. As we continue to do this, we just keep creating and re-creating what we don't want. If your life were ideal, what would it look like? How would it feel? Make a list of one hundred things that describe "My Ideal Life." Imagine parts of your list every day as if it were real, with a thankful heart, and guess what will be showing up for you?

9. Choose to be happy rather than right. Forget about rightness and go for the happiness. Practice saying a lot, *It doesn't matter!* The more you choose to feel good, the faster your desires show up for you.

10. Pray. Ask God to energize your belief. God's grace is free for the asking. It is pure, powerful energy available to anyone. If your belief is a 4, ask God to take it to a 10. God's grace will flow to you and energize your faith so you can attract into your life what you have desired and asked for. It is the most powerful energy we have available to us and it is free. Ask away!

All of the above help energize your beliefs with positive emotion. As you hold your belief at a 10, you transmit a powerful vibration to the Universe that opens the flow of receiving what you want. When your beliefs are flat and weak, your desires are slow in coming. When your belief is packed full of enthusiasm, you transmit a high vibration that easily and effortlessly draws into your life what you have asked for. I would love to hear about all of your successes in using all or any of the above techniques. Share your success and it will help others create more of their own.

CHAPTER 32

Your Child May Be a Highly Evolved Master Being

Children today are very different from my generation and earlier. They are very acute to things of a spiritual nature and many are already functioning in their spiritual gifts. They are here to assist the planet in becoming a heaven on earth: a place where gods dwell. They are gods, so essentially they are here to prepare their future home. As their parents, we have the stewardship of supporting them in fine-tuning their spiritual gifts and making sure we do not stifle them and shut them down. As their parents, we can learn to become their spiritual partners as well as their parents, so that we can dwell with them as we prepare ourselves to live in such a glorified space—because we are potential gods as well.

I have witnessed many parents at odds with knowing how to raise these children. They have been conditioned to turn to the medical establishment for answers and the answers have been limited. As a society we have labeled many of these children as mentally ill and hyperactive too often. We have medicated them to alter their behavior patterns too easily. We have seen them as the problem when we, the adults, have been the problem. We have created categories to shove these children into such as

Attention Deficit Disorder, Attention Deficit Hyperactivity Disorder, problem children, behavior-challenged, autistic, or just simply hard to handle. The bottom line is that because of their spiritual gifts and qualities, they experience this world differently than the adults in it; although we keep trying to make them like us. It will never happen. They are very strong and we cannot change them. At a cellular level they know who they are and will not abandon this knowledge. They will make it through the maze we keep putting in their way and come out the other side intact. They will not miss out on much—it is the parents of these marvelous children who are missing out.

By parenting in the old energy, you are missing out on creating a spiritual partnership and friendship with someone you have known and revered for a very long time. You are missing out on openly inviting a powerful spiritual force and energy, to which these children are connected, into your home to because you keep trying to shut it down or alter it.

A young mother brought her eight-year-old son to me to have me help him. I knew from her description of him over the phone that he was a very enlightened and spiritually gifted child. She shared that they had seen several doctors and specialists to try and diagnose what was wrong with him. He was close to being diagnosed as schizophrenic and chronically hyperactive and being sent out of state to be treated by another specialist.

At his appointment, I very candidly asked him if he ever saw things from above him. He very matter of factly told me that just the other day he was out of his body above himself watching two boys on his school playground fight over a ball and how silly he thought that was. I asked him if he saw colors around people and he told me, yes, and that I had blue around me at that moment. His mother, astonished, asked him what color she was. He replied, "You are always changing, Mom, you're different colors all the time." I attempted to explain to his mother that her son was not mentally ill. He was experiencing some very advanced spiritual gifts and abilities at a very young age.

This young boy is empathic with very strong spiritual senses. He has psychic skills without the guidance of how to appropriately use them and continue to develop them. I knew it, he knew it, and we were both fine with talking about it. I knew who he was spiritually, and I was able to acknowledge him that day.

Within the week, I spoke with his mom and she had shared with her husband my explanations of what was going on with their son. The father was not able to accept this, fearing it was evil, and still believing that they needed to fix their son because he was ill. They had decided to send him to the next specialist to continue their search of trying to find out what was "wrong" with him.

Deep down I knew this young boy would ultimately be okay. He was so advanced spiritually, there was nothing that they would be able to do to shut him down completely. God reassured me this was his path and much good would evolve eventually as he would grow up to teach and influence others firsthand to accept children like him. It was confirmed to me that his brief meeting with me was enough of the acknowledgement he was looking for, for him to stay anchored to his truth. I knew he would be okay amidst the drama of his parents. He would eventually move on into his own path, free to be himself, and his spirit support would bring him through his conflict-ridden childhood. The people who were missing out on blessings were his parents. To have a child of such profound spiritual capacities is an awesome gift. Most of the spirits coming in at this time are spiritually advanced. Prepare yourself and your space to raise your children in such a manner that you can be a recipient of the blessings and spiritual energies they bring in.

The Millennial Grandchild

The year is 2020. My four children have all married and I am the delighted grandmother of several grandchildren. I am pleased that my grandchildren are growing up with a deeper knowledge of who they are and an awareness of their spiritual gifts and intuitive abilities.

The earth has increased in its vibrational frequency and so have the people on it. We are a more spiritually evolved, enlightened, and compassionate people. We understand that at the finest levels of our being, we are a system of energy. We are actually vessels of light and sound. We no longer look at a person as a physical body; we see the physical body as a vehicle that also incorporates emotional, mental, and spiritual bodies. We have awakened to our spiritual blueprint—the information that lies at the fundamental level of our being, guiding us as life unfolds. We understand that disharmony and ill health result from negative energy accumulation, energy blockages, and old patterns clouding and distorting the blueprints and instructions for manifesting optimal health. We use technologies and therapies to quickly and easily clear and remove the negative energy, blocks, and patterns in the system.

My grandchildren ask me in amazement why we used to medicate children or classify them as mentally ill because their vibrational frequency was higher than their parents' and because they were spiritually advanced. They find it interesting that I grew up in a time when very few people talked openly about their spiritual abilities and intuitive gifts. I tell them we used to use terms like psychotic, hallucinogenic, schizophrenic, hyperactive, autistic, and attention deficit with people who were actually very evolved and connected with their extrasensory perceptions and spiritual powers. My grandchildren relate to words like intuitive, empathic, precognitive, and visionary, which we use now to describe an individual with highly developed spiritual senses.

We acknowledge how grateful we are to live in a time when there are no more labels and we have embraced our true capacity for wellness, joy, and unconditional love.

KNOWLEDGE HAS ORGANIZING POWER INHERENT IN IT

The following statement by Deepak Chopra woke me up to how easy it can be to change our lives. I realized I was working harder than I needed to, expecting clients to work harder than they needed to. He wrote:

"Using effort to consciously practice an attitude or to cultivate a mood is unnecessary and can cause stress and strain. It is important only that we know what [the] attitudes are, ... that we be aware of them. The more we become aware of them, the more this knowledge gets structured in our consciousness and awareness. Then it is more likely that our attitude and behavior will change spontaneously, without any effort on our part.

Knowledge has organizing power inherent in it. It is simply enough to know, to be aware of the principles; the knowledge will be processed and metabolized by our bodies, and the results will be spontaneous. The results do not occur overnight, but begin to manifest gradually over a period of time." [17]

What I believe Dr. Chopra is teaching us is that all we have to do to change our attitudes and behavior is to repeatedly

---

[17] Deepak Chopra. *The A to Z Steps to a Richer Life*. New York, NY: Barnes and Noble. 1993. pp.1-2.

put our attention on the principles and knowledge we want to awaken to. By listening daily to or reading the truths we want to incorporate into our lives, we will receive the benefit of our lives changing *spontaneously* and *effortlessly*.

As humans we think we have to put in a certain amount of effort for real change to occur. To just read lists or listen to tapes and then go on with our day seems too simple. Again we are faced with the belief that in order to be a recipient of something good, we must earn it or go through a struggle to be worthy of it.

Consider the possibility that any knowledge that rings true to you already exists within you, that within the *intelligence of your cells* is the energy that represents this truth. As you continue to give daily attention to it by reading it or listening to it, it will be woven into your consciousness as thought and behavior and *you will become it*.

Anything you believe and feel is spiritual truth is something you are remembering. We remember spiritual truth rather than find it. Spiritual truth is held within each of us as the light of Christ that resonates as a vital part of our biology. By giving attention to spiritual truths, by reading them or listening to them daily, we awaken this truth in all our parts. It is as if our body is a big mansion with a lot of dark rooms. When truth is remembered, it is as if the lights are being turned on in more rooms. We each have the potential to have all our lights turned on, to vibrate and biologically function as Christ did. As we put our attention on spiritual truth and knowledge, we are activating more of our DNA strands and more of our brain becomes operative.

List the affirmations and intentions that you want to manifest in your life. I spend time in each session helping my clients create lists and scripts that they can read daily to assist them in awakening these attitudes and behaviors. I have witnessed real and lasting change occur effortlessly for many people as they have put this into daily practice.

Read the following script daily and watch your life change:

It's amazing how well my day goes. It is as if the Universe knows who I am and what I want and things flow to me in such a timely way. It is as if I'm dancing with the Universe.

Emergencies are nonexistent in my physical experience. The people that come to me are benefiting by their exposure to me. It is as if I have a secretary in the sky that is taking care of everything and just feeding it to me with such ease and grace and comfort that my day just flows and unfolds so magnificently.

When I wake up in the morning, I am infused with the energy of well-being. I'm just glad to be alive. I can hardly wait to exercise my body and I am thankful for the time I can spend with my children.

When they awaken, my children and spouse are joyful and happy to be alive and we have such fun interacting with one another. This is some of the most precious time of our day as we embark upon our day together—positively anticipating what will unfold.

As I am making my way to different events of my day, it is always such a lovely time. I am so appreciative of all the wonderful people I have in my life. I am grateful for the spiritual support and the angelic help that is taking care of the details and making sure that this day is going to unfold in a magical way.

I love seeing their attention to detail, and I love seeing them eagerly finding more ways to make everything go comfortably. I love recognizing that they're helping me bring my life into balance.

I love being a wife/husband. I love being a mom/dad. I love getting into a space wherein I realize that I can deal with anything. I love connecting with the infinite power and knowledge of my life. I love knowing the benefit I offer to others. Most of all, I love the joy of the unfolding. I love new surprises that come, my ability to move with them, and the inspiration that comes to me effortlessly. I love knowing that I can participate in anything I want to participate in. I love knowing I have infinite choices.

Tell the Universe the way you want it to be! Even if you have to stretch it a little bit. The Universe doesn't know the difference.

CHAPTER 34

THE PURPOSE OF THE PLANET

We are living in a unique time. Life is changing as we know it. Time is going faster. We are at the threshold of this planet becoming a heaven on earth. What if the planet Earth was created as a cosmic spiritual experiment? The gods got together to create a plan that would advance all of God's children on all of his planets with earth being the proxy. What if earth fell from a place of light farther than any other planet ever has, so the beings that came to earth could experience the biggest dynamic of contrast and laws of opposition of any planet created?

Maybe if Christ had gone to any of the other worlds God has created, he would have been loved and accepted and never crucified. Yet his atoning sacrifice was a critical act on behalf of all of God's children everywhere. It was necessary to ensure immortality for everyone. In that case, evil has served a great role and purpose in the universal scheme of things. Satan has been playing a very critical role by holding and orchestrating the dark energies that have functioned on the earth. That role is almost complete. As we each come to joy through knowing pain, we can graduate from pain being the means to know joy. We live in a time when we can each, individually, bind Satan from having any influence over us. As we do this one-by-one, we are free to experience joy free of any pain. We can grow in joy and learn in love.

There have been some books published in the last several years that have gotten much attention by espousing that there is no Satan, that we created this myth from our attachment to fear. Also, in most metaphysical writings, Christ is seen as an ascended master with no reference to his being our Savior. I believe there is a Satan and Christ is our Savior, and all other ascended masters know this. Christ stands on the right hand of God—resurrected beings in physical bodies that have been transfigured and glorified. Satan is one of God's spirit children as well, Christ's spiritual brother who opted to not receive a body and chose to play a role in the drama of the earth's journey by tempting us and trying us so we could come to know good from evil. Satan does his job really well; he is very committed. How committed are you to fulfilling what you came to earth to receive a body and be and do?

We Lived As Spirits before We Came to Earth

We existed as spirits before we came to earth. We lived as spirit children with our Heavenly Father and Heavenly Mother who created our spirit bodies from spiritual matter or intelligence. We have no beginning and we have no end; we are eternal in our nature because we were created from eternal material. Our spirit bodies were created in the image of God. I believe God is a perfect being with a resurrected body of flesh and bone. He has acquired the spiritual status as a physical being that we have the same potential to be. God is not only a superior intelligence that permeates the Universe, he is also a tangible body of flesh and bones that is perfect. His spirit emanates throughout the entire Universe: it's everywhere and in everything. God wants us to become like him.

In the spirit realm we were all endowed with agency and the capacity to choose for ourselves. We were presented with a plan and given the opportunity to choose if we wanted to participate in the plan. The plan was to create a planet of free choice and to go down to it and receive a physical body. We would be in a world of contrast: good and evil would be the two forces that would influence our every choice.

The Father's plan was for us to prevail over the evil and come to know our God-self and our powers for creating good in this lifetime. In the spirit realm, we were given the choice to follow one of our two spirit brothers: one that represented the dark energy, and the other who represented the light. Those who chose to follow the being of light were given the promise of being endowed with a physical body. Those who followed the being of dark left the spirit realm as spirits to coexist with the physical beings on earth to fulfill the role of tempting and trying us in our quest to become like God.

When I see a client for the first time, I assist them with guided imagery in creating as best they can a recollection of living in the light before their birth. In every cell of our body is our intelligence. Within that intelligence we hold the energy of every existence and of every experience we have ever had. By going into an alpha-theta brainwave state, we tap into our inner world that holds our knowledge and cellular memory. In the Rapid Eye Technology (RET) process you are in an alpha-theta state and able to tap into all that is held in the deeper mind and body.

As clients have called forth this knowledge, they have discovered that they didn't always feel 100 percent confident in coming to earth. Frequently, people have carried into this life feelings of inferiority, confusion, fear, anger, discouragement, and doubt. Some have felt tremendous grief for the spirits they left behind or for those who chose not to come to earth at this time. They are unaware that they have been trying to process these feelings and clear them for most of their lives.

Most people experience change as difficult and challenging. They resist it and try to avoid it. One of the biggest changes we each encountered was to leave a spirit realm and take on a physical body. In the prebirth clearing process, we are clearing the subconscious beliefs and energy residues of many of the following deeper beliefs that are still interfering with our moving forward and progressing in life:

❖ Feelings of not being ready, hesitant.

❖ Afraid I won't get back to the light. What if I fail?

❖ Feeling inadequate, out of control.

❖ Regret.

❖ A physical body is dangerous; humans are dangerous.

❖ Feeling too small and weak to live.

❖ Sad I made the wrong choice.

❖ Sad I am leaving God and the ones I love.

❖ Not ready to leave.

❖ Overwhelmed, disconnected, insecure, and unsafe.

❖ Angry about the parents I have chosen.

❖ Going to the wrong family; I wanted a different family.

For most people, every time they are faced with life-changing decisions, these energies and subconscious beliefs are triggered. We are faced with choosing to move through them, which aids us in clearing them, but if we do not, we are honoring them, which keeps us stuck. With RET these beliefs are cleared easily and effectively from the deepest level, freeing a person to move forward—allowing change with little or no resistance at all. We are supported in experiencing more and more synchronicity and miracles in our life when we clear old energies, and trust and let God lead us as we create a new life.

I frequently work with clients who are carrying residual anger about the parents and families they came to and the life challenges they are suffering. They perceive God as having assigned them these lots in life, and they feel they were never given a choice. This perception sets God up to be disinterested in them and using them to his benefit. Too many people feel used and ignored by God, and yet they are afraid to turn away from him out of fear of receiving more doom and gloom in their lives. As they clear this perceived negativity from their deeper perspective, they begin to remember the choices they made and how perfectly it has all played out for their growth and learning. They begin to connect with the real God, which allows them to start praying more and asking for what they want, knowing that God loves them and wants as much joy and happiness for them as he does anyone else.

Occasionally, I work with a client that is suffering from a hidden death wish. At a very deep level they have not committed 100 percent to being here on the earth. They are unaware why they feel overwhelmed and incapable of being successful. At a deeper level they seem to be questioning the decision they made as a spirit to come. Once we have identified this connection, I explain to them that they have several choices. They can keep experiencing life in regret and apathy, they can clear their fear and choose again—this time creating the belief that they want to be here and will be successful, or they can return to spirit. Everyone I have worked with has chosen to clear his or her fears and choose again. This is easily accomplished by having the client imagine him or herself in the light that they existed in before their birth. Since there is no past, present, and future to spirit, whatever we put our attention on becomes our present. From this point they are ready to clear their fears and insecurities about coming to earth. After the clearing they can create new beliefs like the following:

- ❖ I am comfortable moving forward with my life.
- ❖ I am successful.
- ❖ I am experiencing change that comes easily to me.
- ❖ I am glad I am alive; life is a wonderful surprise.
- ❖ I am experiencing a physical body that is safe and comfortable.
- ❖ I am happy and healthy.
- ❖ I am committed to being here.
- ❖ I am making a difference.

The clients' intentions are honored and it is as if they have always held these beliefs. Their life changes and soon reflects back to them what they now believe about themselves.

Several of my clients had been suicidal and either thought about or attempted to take their lives before they started working with me. I have discovered that they are really not interested in ending their lives. Individuals that are suicidal feel trapped and powerless. They feel stuck in a tremendous amount of pain—a very, very heavy energy that can be difficult to clear without assistance. What they really want is relief from this all-consuming heavy energy and they believe taking their life is the only escape. They believe they have no other choices that will create a feeling of safety and freedom in their lives.

Their perception of the world is that it is not a safe place and they are complete victims to random events that continue to pull them down. They believe that the only choice they have left that would free them of their misery would be to stop living—which would release them from their pain.

Rather then trying to talk them out of suicide, I tell them they still have that choice. I honor their right to choose what they think they want. This honors the individual and sends the message that they are not powerless. Honoring that they have a choice to end their life actually keeps them alive. By believing they actually have a choice they are less likely to act on it. All they were looking for was some sense of freedom. As they clear their fears and false beliefs about themselves and the world they live in, they begin to believe in other choices. As the negative energies are cleared and more and more light is restored within them, they are able to move into a perception that life is worth living. They begin to change their perception about themselves and the world, which changes the events and the people they attract into their lives.

At the end of the prebirth clearing process, as clients imagine themselves in the light, I tell them to look around at all the spiritual support that is available to them. If they tell me there is none, I ask them if they want to keep experiencing their earthly journey alone or would they like some spiritual support and help now. They always want the help. We call in beings of light, ministering angels from on high, and I have the person imagine being surrounded by this spiritual support. Not just as a spirit in Heaven, but as a human walking the earth with angels that go before them and walk with them on their right, on their left, and behind them.

By going back in your mind to the light before your birth, you are able to connect with a fundamental aspect of your whole self. Many things play into our current experience. I have found that clearing our perceptions of our spirits' insecurities and fears frees us to move forward with more grace and success in our current life.

⌒

Janet had very little self-esteem and feelings of self-worth. She had been married three times to abusive men. She had been repeatedly physically abused by her mother and had an emotionally absentee father. She had a distinct memory from her teenage years of standing in the kitchen with her mother and her mother saying to her, "I don't know why any man would want to love you." Her inner-children were still believing these core beliefs: *Everyone I love the most and I want to love me, end up hurting me,* and *I can never do anything good enough to be loved.* These beliefs emanated so powerfully from her that she kept sending out a signal that attracted abusive men into her life. She also worked in a job that was paying her less than her real worth. She struggled to make ends meet as a single mother and kept recreating a life of lack. She had a lack of love, a lack of money, a lack of time, and a lack of support. She had difficulty believing that God really loved her and that he was interested in her. This kept her from prayerfully asking for help for her desires in life because she was projecting onto God that he really didn't care about her.

At the beginning of her session, I asked her if she had ever felt the love God had for her. She could not remember ever experiencing it. Although intellectually she knew God loved her, she had never actually felt the love he had for her. I instructed her to speak an intention that would allow this to happen in her life. The intention she spoke was, "I am knowing and feeling the love God has for me. I am trusting that I am important to him and he is there for me."

Toward the end of her first session, I told Janet to imagine herself in the light with Jesus Christ. Christ was there with someone who wanted to meet her and loved her very much. Christ brought forth Heavenly Father who received her into his arms. At this point she began to weep as she described a feeling that washed through her and over her: the energy of unconditional love that her Father in Heaven has for her. I distinctly felt it come into the room at the same moment she did. I have felt this with several clients, and I feel I am to be a second witness so they will not doubt it. I am brought to tears with them and we both know a miracle has occurred and it is a familiar feeling—one they once knew and are now remembering.

⌢

It is fascinating to help people reconnect with their spiritual origins and to help them clear deep-level inhibitions and negative feelings that have been interfering with their entire life. It is a profound experience to assist someone in reconnecting with their spiritual roots, their spiritual support system, and their first parents—Heavenly Father and Mother—one for which I hold a tremendous reverence. I ask for miracles to occur in the lives of my clients. I am getting used to how fast these requests are honored.

$\mathcal{E}$ACH OF US HAS SPIRITUAL BROTHERS AND SISTERS WHO ARE NOT IN OUR BIOLOGICAL FAMILY

Have you ever met someone and felt that you have always known them? A strong connection and a feeling of familiarity prevails as you are together. Since we are all spirit children of our Heavenly Father and Mother, we are all spirit brothers and sisters. Why do we feel a closer draw to some people but not to everyone? Maybe we were created in family groups and these family groups go beyond our biological families. Maybe our spiritual birth order is closer to these people than to others. Maybe we were involved in each other's preparation and planning to come to earth.

There will be some people you will meet that will get your attention, and you will be strongly attracted to them. Maybe you feel more whole and complete when you are with them, and you yearn to be in their company. Their role for us is to mirror back to us portions of ourselves that we have forgotten. The energy of their beings is helping awaken our own spiritual virtues, qualities, and characteristics. Consider that the love and connection you feel with them is really the love you have for yourself and the desire to know your wholeness once again.

While attending a training seminar, I met a gentleman with whom I had a very strong connection. We both agreed it felt like we were being reunited as long-lost brother and sister. We communicated easily and spoke about intimate details of our lives that two people just meeting do not usually discuss. The feeling of love and support made it easy. The feelings were not romantic; it was distinctly a feeling of family. The last day of our training, we both showed up in yellow shirts, blue jeans, brown belts, and the same-colored socks. We were dressed identically, without consciously intending to do so. We looked at each other and laughed at how the spirit likes to play tricks with us.

Even though our connection as close spirit brother and sister was very distinct, it didn't mean we were meant to keep in close contact the rest of our lives once we reunited here. We were influential with each other that week and had contact for a brief period thereafter. Our paths have not crossed recently. Neither of us feel the need because we are both busy in our own purposes.

Understanding our spiritual relationship with others helps us make wise choices and manage these relationships with integrity. Gregg Braden counsels us,

"For some individuals, having these feelings of attraction without understanding the mirror may seem awkward or inappropriate. You may even believe that you are in love and feel all the guilt of the inappropriateness of the encounter. Knowing what your feelings are saying to you will allow you to act consciously, rather than following some mysterious and compelling force that you cannot explain."[18]

To help you manage these encounters with integrity, say to yourself, *This other person that I find myself drawn to is my*

---

[18] Gregg Braden. *Walking Between the Worlds.* Bellevue, WA: Radio Bookstore Press. 1997. pg. 9.

spiritual brother or sister. I am noticing in them spiritual qualities and characteristics of myself that have been dormant in me. That is what I am attracted to. I claim these parts of myself and ask the Holy Spirit to awaken and integrate them within me.

We are all spiritual siblings, and everyone on earth is our spiritual family. Knowing that we knew many spirits intimately before we came to earth is a powerful insight to guide us in our interactions and choices as we meet people to whom we are closely drawn. In this knowledge, we can choose to properly manage ourselves free of jeopardizing other close relationships that we have developed in our lives.

We All Made Sacred Agreements Before We Came to Earth

As spirits in the spirit realm we each had an opportunity to design our physical experience. I like to think God and Jesus Christ, as well as other beings of light, assisted us in this process. We knew there would be outcomes to achieve, lessons to learn, and knowledge of truth to acquire. We needed others to show up to play out certain roles for us, and we also made agreements to show up for others.

With many of the clients I have assisted, I have felt a prior association as spirits. Numerous times as I met with and helped them, there was unspoken communication wherein I said, "I told you I would prepare myself so I could help you. Thanks for showing up, trusting me, and giving me the chance."

In the movie, *Simon Birch,* Simon is a boy of twelve with serious special needs. His most obvious difference is that he isn't more than two-and-a-half feet tall. He believes that there is a spiritual purpose in his extra-small size. He claims, "I believe God has a plan for me. I believe God is going to use me as an instrument on his behalf."

I believe God's plan for each of us is the plan we designed for ourselves with his help. Each of us is a child of God. He gave us each individual attention in helping create a plan that would be harmonious with our spiritual abilities and acquired biological and generational inheritances. The purpose of each of our plans is to awaken us to our God-self, to obtain spiritual mastery of our creative powers, and to use our powers as a creator to bless our lives and others' lives by creating more of what brings joy.

In the design of our plan, we each made sacred agreements and contracts with God. These are not spiritual have-to's, need-to's, or should's by which we are bound. God is not a power-hungry, controlling, authoritarian who demands that we follow through with what we agreed to participate in. He desires that we be successful in playing out and completing our contracts because we will be the greatest benefactors. We receive the spiritual growth and the advancement into more levels of light and truth.

God has a plan for this earth and all those who have dwelled on it. His plan involves bringing to pass the immortality and eternal life of mankind and advancing this planet into a glorified state. Each of our own plans and contracts involve assisting him in ways that are perfectly suited for our gifts, abilities, nature, and desires. The success of God's plan is not dependent on us. There is always someone to replace us if we fail to fulfill our contracts.

Does God love us any less if we choose out? I believe not. God has complete allowing and unconditional love for each of us, no matter what we do. If we fail to live a higher level of spirituality or choose out of our contracts, we deny ourselves blessings. We are not loved any less; we have just chosen a different experience.

To be benefactors of more levels of light and spiritual advancement, we are required to live higher laws. That is the purpose of commandments, sacred covenants, contracts, and agreements. How do you know what contracts you made as a spirit? Ask.

Remember, "Ask, and it shall be given you; seek, and ye shall find; knock, and it shall be opened unto you."[19] A prayer as simple as:

Dear God, thank you for revealing to my conscious mind what my spiritual agreements and contracts are. I desire to be engaged in them and to create successful outcomes so that I am an instrument in thy hands to bless my life and others'.

How will you know when you are about to come into the playing out of a contract? In most cases, you feel compelled to be a part of something that connects with you very deeply. You can't ignore it, although in some cases, it may seem irrational. Like most people, you may try to resist the promptings coming to you with excuses and logical reasons not to move forward.

At the threshold of initiating a contract you will experience opposition. It is this way with all things in the physical dimension. The opposition you will be faced with will most likely be the feeling of fear or inadequacy. The Universe is offering you this experience as a rite of passage to qualify you for your contract. As you pass through the energy of fear and engage in the role of playing out your sacred agreements, you ignite energy and open up the blueprint of your contract.

---

[19] Luke 11:9.

The details and design of your spiritual agreements have already been created. Your role is to hold the intention and to let the energy flow through you to activate physical manifestations and experiences. As you do this, you will receive clear guidance and instruction on what to think and do. As you continue to ask the heavens to orchestrate the details, the people and events will flow to you effortlessly.

There are many different contracts and agreements. They are as unique as our individual vibrations and spiritual character. For some it may be as simple as knowing their truth, and staying in their light so their light vibration is networked into and received by the collective consciousness of humanity. I tell each of my clients, "All of humanity is blessed by your existence here on the earth. There is nothing you even have to do to bless the lives of others. As you act as your true self and let your light shine, your unique vibration makes the world a better place for everyone in it."

For many people, their contracts include assisting in the clearing of their family lineage of disharmonious and negative beliefs and patterns. In order to fulfill this, they planned to come into dysfunctional families. For some, illness may be their contract. A child with cancer is a great teacher of spiritual strength and tenacity. The child plays a role in the lives of many to support them in awakening their Christ-selves.

Your spiritual contracts may be quiet and obtuse or they may be visual and obvious to many. Or they may include both kinds. Either way, you bless the lives of many more than you are aware of. Based on the principle of when you affect one, you affect many because we are all connected, you cannot help shifting the entire Universe when you bless the life of one. Spiritual contracts always involve helping one or many remember their Christ-selves and their infinite worth. In doing this, we help others graduate into their divine role as a son or daughter of God. The people we affect are more free to fulfill their contracts. We help others complete the recovery and healing segments of their lives so they can come into the intention and creating segments.

I believe our children—the adults of the next millennium—have contracts that are unique to the time in which we live. Their contracts may involve assisting in the winding-down scenes and preparing the planet and the people on it to receive Christ. When he comes, the light level of the earth's occupants will be such that "every knee shall bow, and every tongue shall confess"[20] that Jesus is the Christ and Savior of this world. At that time there will be many whose contracts involve assisting Christ in creating a Christ Community.

God does have a plan for this world. God offered us a unique opportunity to participate consciously with him in executing this plan. He wants each of us to rise to as much spiritual capacity as we can in our lives. He loves us no less if we choose more or choose less. Through the power of his grace offered to us in the energy of the Atonement, he will match and surpass what our own intentions give power to. He wants us each to create as much success as possible; he compares us with no one.

It really is up to you. What do you want to experience? What do you want to acquire spiritually? Don't be so hard on yourself. Have more fun and be more playful with all of this. It is meant to bring us joy now, not just a byproduct of joy later.

---

[20] Doctrine and Covenants 88:104.

If you were to look back through the ancestors that came before you, you would most likely be able to identify generational patterns that are still playing out in your life. Maybe there has been abuse and victims for several generations, or maybe poverty consciousness, low self-esteem and depression, abandonment and neglect, feelings of not being good enough, of incompetence, or a history of addictions and making things harder than they need to be.

Whatever the dysfunctional pattern, your life may have the magnified version of them so you would take notice and do something about it. You needed these patterns to be magnified so you wouldn't forget the important role you agreed to play for your family and for all of humanity. If you have not taken care of it in your lifetime, your children will be given the same opportunity and will most likely have the same patterns magnified more in their life experience. As you clear these patterns, you are free to create new healthy beliefs and patterns to pass on to your posterity. You have become a transition person or, in Carlfred Broderick's words, a *Savior on Mount Zion:*

"My profession as a family therapist has convinced me that God actively intervenes in some destructive lineages, assigning a valiant spirit to break the chain of destruction in such families. Although these children may suffer innocently as victims of violence, neglect, and exploitation, through the grace of God some find the strength to metabolize the poison within themselves, refusing to pass it on to future generations of destructive pain; after them the line flows clear and pure. Their children and children's children will call them blessed.

In suffering innocently that others might not suffer, such a person, in some degree, becomes a 'Savior on Mount Zion' by helping to bring salvation to a lineage.

In a former era, the Lord sent a flood to destroy unworthy lineages. In this generation, it is my faith that he has sent numerous choice individuals to help purify them."[21]

It is my personal belief that in our spirit life before our birth, many individuals agreed to come to families with the purpose of interrupting the generational sins and dysfunctions of their family line. Many made sacred agreements and received instruction to prepare them to come forth in the due time of the Lord to labor in his vineyard for the salvation of the souls of men.

Many are tired of the family sickness that they have witnessed and experienced. They are tired of passing it on to their own children. They believe their children deserve more, and in order for them to offer more, it has been required of them to face and change the patterns of dysfunction and to clear all the emotional baggage that has been passed on from generations preceding them.

As a transition person, you are awakening healthier ways to take care of yourself and healthier ways to parent. By healing yourself, you are rebuilding the old waste places to "raise up

[21] Carlfred Broderick. *Saviors on Mount Zion*. Ensign. Salt Lake City, UT: Aug. 1986. pg. 38.

foundations of many generations to be called the repairer of the breach, the restorer of paths to dwell in."[22] We are a chosen generation, which has been called out of darkness to receive Christ's marvelous light in order to help prepare the earth for his return.

⌒

The first time I met Karla she was pushed into my office in a wheelchair in a state of numbness due to all the medication she was taking. She had been in and out of mental hospitals the last ten years, was considered mentally ill, and had been diagnosed with Disassociate Identity Disorder (DID). Doctors had told her that she might experience some recovery by her late forties. At the time I met her she was twenty-nine. She was married and had no children. Due to the extreme sexual and ritual abuse she experienced as a child, she would never be able to have her own biological children. I sensed that Karla had not only taken on the negative energies from her family's dysfunction, she seemed also to have taken on the residual energy of abuse for much of humanity.

Disassociate Identity Disorder is a fascinating condition. Our minds have the capacity to split and create another identity that can be so developed that it no longer has a connection consciously with our core personality. In the case of extreme trauma in childhood, many people disassociate and create other identities so the core personality feels like it is no longer present—creating a sense of safety. The personalities that are

---

[22] Isaiah 58:12.

created have the primary function of protecting and keeping the core personality alive. Little by little, the world is perceived to be more and more dangerous, and the core belief is, *No one can be trusted, especially those who appear to love me the most. They will hurt me the most.* As complicated as it appears, it is really one of the easiest disorders to work with because the client has created an extremely organized defense system rooted at the subconscious level.

As a result of trial and error in working with Karla and numerous other clients that came to me with DID, I found out that I would not see any success until I had a rapport with and trust from the key personalities that had been created to protect her real self.

Our first task was to find out who was in charge of Karla's system. There is always a protector and a gatekeeper. I find it fascinating that everyone I work with who has DID understands these titles and the jobs associated with them. It is as if there were a universal language understood by the subconscious mind that all my clients with this disorder connected with immediately. In Karla's case there were about twenty-five core personalities with four in charge. At deeper levels we found hundreds that were identified as pain-holders, emotion-holders, babies, cutters, messengers, record-keepers, and sleepers. Underneath those personalities there was what I called a sea of negative energy that was in total chaos. Karla's core personality was hardly ever present in her day-to-day life. She had been programmed heavily to believe that she would just have to endure this life of fear. I remember distinctly my first session with Karla. I was experiencing her shifting into different personality states that all wanted to check me out. It was overwhelming and exhausting. We just kept clearing the negative emotions.

I told her I wanted to speak to her most spiritual, higher self. The room became very quiet and she looked straight at me and said, "Yes?" I asked her if it was time for the healing to occur. She told me it was, and in that moment I felt a wave of compassion wash through me, and a spiritual memory flashed through my mind of being in the light before our birth together and promising her that I would help her reclaim her true essence. There were many times in the upcoming months when that sacred agreement kept me going when I wondered if we were making any headway.

I seem to have great success with very difficult clients. I respond to them with tough love—being very firm, direct, confident, and very, very loving at the same time. I don't allow them to play their games with me. I help them take ownership of their lives, and I never judge them. As a result of this, Karla's personalities became very fond of me and wanted a lot of contact with me. This was a new experience, being able to trust someone and let someone help them and love them.

After a couple of sessions I started receiving phone calls at my home from Karla—not just one or two but twenty to thirty a day. We discussed this. I told her if she wanted to keep seeing me she had to agree to not call me, and I had her sign an agreement. Nothing changed, and it even became worse. If I wasn't there, she wouldn't believe my children and would tell them if they didn't get me she was going to drown herself in the creek. One of her patterns was to scare people so they would give her what she wanted. She believed very deeply that she would never have anything she wanted because she didn't deserve it. I told my children not to worry about her and to tell her, "Thank you for keeping your agreement not to call. We love you. Good-bye," and then to hang up.

After a couple more weeks of this pattern I realized why she wasn't keeping her agreement. It was because not all of the personalities had agreed. The ones who were calling were not the ones that were "up" when we discussed this. It was a great scapegoat mechanism that could be used to avoid accountability with many of her dysfunctional patterns. When I discussed this with her, sure enough only a couple had made the agreement and all the others believed they were free to call.

I was inspired to hold a conference of all the dissociated parts inside Karla. I asked for them all to assemble in a safe place, and I asked for a satellite system to be set up. We created a big screen theater and Karla's eyes were the satellite that carried the information from the outside world into the internal camera to project it onto the screen for all to see. With everyone in attendance, I asked them all to agree to stop calling me. I agreed to call her a couple of times between sessions to see how everyone was doing. They all made the agreement and stuck to it.

Assisting Karla was one of the biggest adventures of my career. We both worked very hard and have some amazing stories to tell. When I met her, she was completely dependent on the care of a live-in nurse and was not safe to be alone by herself. Some of her patterns included cutting herself, calling 9-1-1 with contrived emergencies, switching to childlike personalities when she felt threatened, hallucinating, and others. Her sexual relationship with her husband had been non-existent for many years.

Karla saw me twice a week, and within several months we were able to clear and integrate all the per-sonalities back into her original self. It took another year for Karla to acquire her full presence in her adult energy and to gain her independence from a caregiver. Her condition continues to improve. Every time I talk with her she reports another success in her life. It has been several years now since I met her. I recently spoke with her over the phone and found out that she and her husband are foster parents to a two-month-old. They have been told they will be able to adopt their own child within a few months. She and her husband are creating a successful marriage wherein their sexual relationship is now thriving. It wasn't long ago that Karla thought none of this could happen for her.

Karla showed me the power of the human spirit to overcome any level of challenge. I believe we made sacred agreements before we came into this lifetime. Many of those agreements included what would be experienced as overwhelming at times. In the making of those agreements we were also given the blueprint of solutions that would create our capacity to fulfill those agreements. I have met many people who have taken on big assignments on behalf of their biological family and the family of humanity. I know as Karla successfully cleared the layers and layers of energy that had bound her life, she broke an energy ceiling that will now allow others to clear their layers more easily and quickly.

CHAPTER

39

Do You Believe in the Real God?

Everyone has his or her own personal perception of who or what God is. This perception has been influenced by generational beliefs, childhood experiences with adults, religious teachings, and personal experiences with religious and spiritual things throughout our entire life. For many adults, their perceptions of who God is to them is a byproduct of their inner-child's experience with men. Some of the more common deeper beliefs I have helped clients clear include:

- ✦ God is not interested in me.
- ✦ I am not good enough, so I have to be obedient so I at least have a chance at getting back to Heaven.
- ✦ I don't want to burden God with my trivial requests.
- ✦ I am not worthy of what I ask for, so why ask?
- ✦ God doesn't answer my prayers because I am not as important as others, so I don't ask for anything.
- ✦ I am angry with God because he turned his back on me and because so many others have been hurt.

For some individuals, the feelings of worthlessness go beyond their reference to themselves as human beings: they extend into their spiritual identity. I have helped several people clear the subconscious belief that, *I am an inferior spirit. Other spirits are more important than me. I'm not worthy of God's individual attention and assistance in my life.*

Another very common perception is for humans to believe that God is dogmatic, authoritarian, insensitive, and controlling. Much of this is due to all the carnage and inhumanity that has taken place on this planet. If you were abused as a child or have witnessed human trauma, you may have these beliefs about God.

Maggie had been raised in a conventional, religious family. Her father believed in forcing his children to do what was right. Beneath the public persona of a good Christian family were the patterns of emotional, physical, and sexual abuse, acted out repeatedly during her childhood and adolescence.

When I met Maggie, she had abandoned any association with the religion of her childhood several years earlier. As many people do, along with abandoning religion, she had also abandoned all communication with God and any active relationship with Christ and the beings of Heaven. Her perceptions of who God was and what the spirit realm was about were riddled with painful memories of her childhood. In order for her to survive life, she had chosen to shut down any conscious interaction with God and the Heavens.

My goal with clients is to assist them in restoring and bringing into more fullness their connection with their own spirit and the heavens, and to help them reclaim and increase a healthy, trusting relationship with Christ and the real God. In Maggie's case, when it was time to address her spiritual beliefs, I assisted her with the following process:

I asked her to close her eyes and to go to the place where Christ is in the light waiting for her. She saw herself standing in the light with Jesus Christ. I told her to look around and notice all the heavenly beings who were with her in the light and who wanted to assist her. I told her to send two safe and loving beings into her deeper mind to find the eight-year-old Maggie. Once the beings returned with eight-year-old Maggie, the adult Maggie, standing with Christ, received her and told her that everything was okay now. She told her that she was safe and would never have to go back. If it were okay, Christ wanted to give her a hug and tell her how much he loved her. I then instructed Maggie to have her eight-year-old take her and Christ to the place where the God she believed in was.

They came to a place where a very large and ominous being stood unapproachable and frightening. Little Maggie was afraid of this god. I then said, "Have little Maggie ask this big, scary god if he is the real god." I reassured her that he could not lie because Christ was there and he would know if it were a lie. The big, scary god put his head down in shame and said, no. I have done this process with numerous clients and the answer is always, no.

An interesting addition to Maggie's session was that the big, scary god pointed to a curtain behind him. Adult Maggie asked Christ to go and open the curtain. The scene in *The Wizard of Oz,* where the wizard is revealed and a timid, older man behind the curtain is discovered, played out for Maggie. Behind Maggie's curtain, controlling the big, scary god was her dad. In the visualization, her father walked out from behind the curtain a very scared and wounded man. Both Little Maggie and Adult Maggie understood that Dad's anger and control were a facade to protect his wounded inner-child. I suggested that Dad's guardian angels come and escort him out of Maggie's space to his own space where they could help him.

At this point in the process, the fake god was removed. I told Little Maggie and Adult Maggie to turn to Christ because he wanted to introduce them to someone special. I told them to look off into the distance because they were going to see two great lights, side-by-side, coming to meet them. As the two wonderful personages drew closer, I told Maggie to notice how warm, safe, and comfortable she felt, and to let herself feel something she hadn't felt for a very long time—a warming of her soul.

As the beings came to her, she began to recognize their energy. They were her Father and Mother in Heaven. They both gave her a hug and she felt grateful they had shown up, as she welcomed them back into her life.

If you have detached yourself from God or if you are angry with God, then you are at odds with the fake god. The real God is all-loving, all-knowing, all-forgiving, all-perfect, all-powerful, and all-allowing. It is his ability to perfectly allow that has allowed us to come to a planet of free choice and contrast so that we can create and learn through our experiences in order to become more like him.

Invite the real God into your life to be your friend, companion, and partner. Remember that God loves you more than you can comprehend, and he wants you to receive all that he is waiting to offer you. I cannot emphasize this point enough: God loves you, and you are worth all he has to offer. Regardless of your actions, in spite of your weaknesses, you deserve God's love. There are no conditions and nothing you must do to earn it. The love of God, by his very nature of being God, is constant and unchangeable. It is always there for you—no matter what.

How to Have Your Own Conversation with God

We can communicate directly with God at any time. God wants to have a personal, intimate relationship with each of us. Having conversations with God on a regular basis is one of the most powerful and influential ways to bless our lives. We can talk to God about anything. Nothing is too trivial or insignificant in our lives that would be bothersome to God. We can talk to him to seek guidance about all the details of our lives. We can talk to him about our families, our friends, our neighbors, our work, our desires, our dreams, our concerns, and our questions. We can talk to God out loud or in our thoughts. The most common form of communication with God is prayer.

Pray to God in the name of Jesus Christ. Start your prayer by calling upon the father by saying, "Dear God," "Dear Heavenly Father," or "Father in Heaven." Close your prayers in the name of Jesus Christ by saying, "I offer this prayer in the name of Jesus Christ, amen."

A prayer of gratitude is a powerful prayer. When we thank God for what has already occurred in our lives and for what we have asked, we sustain a high level of faith. Most people thank God for what they have already received. Try thanking God for what you want in a manner that shows you believe it is coming. A prayer of pure gratitude would make every expression one of thanks. You might say something like this:

Thank you, God, for watching over me and my loved ones and for keeping us safe this day. Thank you for the good experiences I am going to have today. Thank you for all the money that is coming my way and for my wisdom in using it, and that I am having fun with my experience with it. Thank you for assisting my business in becoming more successful. Thank you for the opportunities that are being orchestrated on my behalf to further my work here on the earth.

Thank you for forgiving me and always loving me. Thank you for always being there for me. Thank you for flowing the energy of the Atonement to me to bless my life this day, and for the power of thy Grace to assist me in being more of who I really am. I love thee and appreciate thee, and say this in the name of Jesus Christ, amen.

As you pray from a place of pure gratitude, you are believing that what you want will be given. As you thank God ahead of time, you are trusting that he loves you and wants to bless your life with that which is desirable to you.

As you close your prayer in the name of Jesus Christ, you seal your offering of gratitude. Your prayer is pure and good and will be honored by God.

Talking to God through prayer is one way to have daily communion with him. Other ways include: visualization, meditation, keeping a journal, and pondering about him in your thoughts throughout your day.

In a meditation or visualization, you can be with God to receive guidance and direction from him. Visualize yourself standing in a place of light in the Heavens. Imagine God standing before you. Since he is your father, he would want to give you a hug. Let him hug you. Imagine God holding you as long as it feels good. Imagine God listening to you as you share what you want to talk to him about. Imagine him responding, counseling, and giving loving feedback.

A conversation is communication with at least two individuals. If you desire to have conversations with God, you will have to pay attention to how he is going to talk back to you. Expect God to reply. Too often people experience prayer as a one-way solicitation to the Heavens without expecting a definite response.

Take time each day to be still and quiet your mind for ten to fifteen minutes. This practice will open and make clearer the channel you have to Heaven. As this channel to Heaven becomes stronger and clearer you will hear the voice of God in your mind and in your heart. He will manifest the truth of all things to you all through your day. The voice of God will speak to you through nature. For example, as you witness a beautiful sunset, you will hear God telling you he loves you and that the sunset is a gift from him. You will hear the voice of God in the works of others. Things people say will ring true to you. They do not know that what they are saying is

God talking through them. You know because you feel it is the answer and guidance for which you have been seeking, what you had previously asked or talked to God about.

Keep a conversations-with-God journal. Write your questions in it and God's responses. The response may not come immediately, but it will come. Write your question and know that you will soon be given the answer. Know that your answer from God will manifest effortlessly and sometimes when least expected in a number of creative ways. As you look back through your journal you will notice that what you used to be unclear about is now very clear to you.

Talk to God all through your day silently in your mind. This silent exchange will sustain you in making choices and behaving in a manner that is harmonious with your core desires.

On a trip to Hawaii, my husband and I were staying on the North Shore of Oahu. It was February, and whales were migrating up to Alaska through the North Shore waters. One morning we joined a small group and sailed out into the waters on a catamaran. The captain told us we would most likely see whales, and we needed to look for the tail, dorsal fin, or spray. About thirty minutes out, others on board started sighting whales. Each time someone sighted a whale I was on the other side of the boat and would miss it. I started talking to God in my mind about this and shared with him that I wanted to see a whale. He told me to ask for this and to have the faith to allow it to happen. In my mind I offered a silent prayer. I said, "Thank you, God, for blessing my life this day with the experience of seeing a whale out here in this beautiful water. This I ask for and give thanks for in the name of Jesus Christ, amen."

I knew that asking God was the first step and that believing it was possible would allow it to happen. I knew if it didn't happen, I either didn't believe enough, or I wanted it so bad my attachment to having this experience actually interfered with allowing it to come forth. So I released any emotional attachment I had and knew it could happen, and if it didn't, I would still feel wonderful and would have a great experience.

About fifteen minutes after my talk with God, I was standing looking to the front of the catamaran when suddenly a humpback whale breached straight up out of the water about one-quarter mile in front of the boat. Then, moments later, he did it again, then a third time, a fourth time, and a fifth time. As we sailed past him we could see his tail flipping out of the water at us, as if he were saying to me, "Thanks for asking!" I knew my conversation with God and my faith allowed that experience to be created. There were people on the catamaran who had been born and raised in Hawaii that had never before witnessed such a spectacular event.

I talk to God a lot every day of my life. I pray formally day and night. I have chats with him all through the day in my mind. I ask for what some people may consider trivial and a waste of God's attention. I know he feels differently. He loves us and wants to bless our lives. He wants us to know real joy, real love, and real compassion. He will speak to you. Start talking and expect answers. Remember to have fun with all of this.

*F*EEL YOUR PRAYERS

Praying with feeling connects us more purely with Heaven. **Feel** what you are praying for transpiring in your life. What would it look like, taste like, sound like, smell like, feel like, if what you were asking for was given?

Recently our family felt impressed to pray for more moisture. A drought situation was developing in our state and we needed the rain to replenish the reservoirs and waterways.

Rather than just praying for rain and snow with my mind, I decided to pray with feeling and to get my body involved in the process. When I asked God to bless us with moisture, I imagined what it would feel like if it were raining. What would it sound like, what would it look like, what would it smell like? I noticed all of those sensations while I was praying. I imagined it starting to rain while I was praying. I imagined I could hear the sounds of raindrops, the smell of fresh rain on the cement, the image of the sky darker with lights on in the house. Well, how did I do? Was my prayer answered? Yes, it has rained and snowed many, many inches since I have been **feeling** my prayers for rain. I am sure others' prayers have been helping as well.

Praying with feeling brings your physical senses into the experience. When we can feel in our body what we are asking for in prayer, we offer a powerful point of attraction for it to show up.

God has told us that faith the size of a mustard seed can move a mountain. I do not know anyone who is seeking to actually move a physical mountain. Yet, we have been endowed with the power to do such if called upon. God has given us the power to command the energy of the elements and, when we believe we can do this, the elements obey us. **Feeling** our prayers gives us this power.

God has not only given us the power to move mountains, He has given us the power to heal our bodies, clear our emotional pain, restore our relationships, create more wealth, and receive anything else we desire and want. Start moving the mountains in your life by feeling your prayers.

In asking God for more rain and moisture, I knew that He was not withholding rain from us. We were withholding it from ourselves. It was not God's decision whether or not we could have rain; it was our decision to ask and receive it. When we ask God to give us what we want or need, we do not need to give him the power of deciding whether or not we can have it. God has given us this power of discernment and the freedom of agency as our tools. Too often we expect Him to decide what it is we should have in our lives. One of God's greatest desires is for us to be aligned with His will. In this position we can only ask for what is in our highest and greatest good.

Sally came to me when she was a single woman, thirty-one years old, never married, and yet yearning to be married. She had resigned herself to being single and felt marriage was not going to happen to her. She had put on a lot of extra weight and felt unattractive and undesirable. She believed that no man would want to marry her because she was "fat", as she described herself. She put losing the weight between herself and marriage, yet her pattern was to feel lonely and depressed and to turn to food for solace and comfort. She felt deprived of marriage and she was not going to deprive herself of food.

She had also given God the power of deciding whether or not she could be married. Her frame of reference was, *I can get married when God brings me my husband. When God decides it's right, I will be able to have it.* We discussed why she had put her marriage experience in God's hands. Why was it up to Him whether or not she married? She really didn't know why. The best she could come up with was, since it is such a big decision, she better let God be in charge of it.

In believing she was undesirable, she created that as her experience. She spent a lot of time alone, rarely meeting anyone or going on dates. As she cleared her fear and negative self-image, she began to lose weight. She decided to believe she was desirable, that she would make a great wife, and that she could attract a great husband. She decided to take back the decision from God and made a choice to become married.

She became aware that as she kept feeling "not married" at the same time she was asking to become married, marriage could not show up easily. Her mountain to move was attracting a worthy, loving partner that she was passionate about marrying. She started to feel her prayers for marriage. What would it feel like to be married to someone she dearly loved? What would it sound like, look like, taste like, smell like? As she prayed with feeling, believing she could start experiencing the sensations of marriage, she was commanding marriage into her life.

She also began to feel the sensations of being lean, fit, and healthy. What does it feel like to be at your ideal weight? What does it look like, sound like, taste like, and smell like? As she put feeling into her prayers for losing weight, she commanded the systems of her body to shed the fat. She started to lose weight easily.

Sally continues to feel her prayers to provide a receiving space for what she is asking to be given. She knows she has great powers, as we all do, to command the elements around us. She desires to be in harmony with God's will to use this power with integrity.

CHAPTER 42

All the Answers Are Inside of Us

If we consider that we came to earth with a spiritual plan stored in the blueprint of our cells, then in that blueprint are the answers and solutions to all of life's questions and challenges.

So often we look outside ourselves to find the spiritual beacon and compass that can steer us on the right course. We each have a spiritual compass to keep us on course and in harmony and rhythm with our plan and purpose. God has implanted in each of us spiritual instruments that are connected with Him that will help guide us home. The light of Christ in each of us is the intelligence that exists within our cells. This energy will guide us home if we will feed it and follow it.

As humans, we have been trained to focus on the problems of life so that we can figure out solutions. However, by focusing on the problems, we are keeping our attention on what we don't want and creating more of it. What we really want to create is an awareness of the answers we are carrying.

In order to focus on the solutions so that you can manifest them, you do not need to know what they are. By putting your thoughts and attention on the belief that a solution is awakening within you, the answers and guidance you are seeking start to form for you consciously.

By focusing on the beliefs—*I am awakening the answers and insights within me that have already been created. I am manifesting them and consciously becoming aware of them. I am making choices that are in harmony with my core desires and spiritual contracts and purpose*—the answers will open and become known to you effortlessly.

Rather than asking God to supply you with the solutions to your life's challenges, ask him to assist you in awakening the answers that lie dormant within you that he helped you create before you came to earth. If one of our objectives were to know our god-self, then God would want us to practice our abilities as creators within our own lives first. It makes sense to me that he would make us agents and stewards over our own lives, creators of our own destiny, before we are graduated to influence in other spheres and dimensions.

As you clear old energies, beliefs, and patterns that are keeping you stuck and asleep to your god-self, you will be free to activate more and more of your spiritual blueprints. At a DNA level of our cells, we each have a blueprint for a life of wholeness and joy: A blueprint for physical wellness, emotional harmony, mental clarity, and spiritual oneness with our higher selves and Christ.

Set an intention to easily and effortlessly awaken the answers, solutions, and insights to your life experiences, and you will. Set an intention to learn your lessons quickly and move into more of your light and truth gracefully. Set an intention to now learn in joy and in your joy continually awaken and integrate your Christ-like self into your physical experience.

Set an intention that you will be one of those called and chosen to help prepare the earth to become a glorified realm where Christ will rule and reign with us. Set an intention that if you are still here when Christ returns, that you will know him because you will be like him.

Stop looking for the answers and understanding of your life outside of you. Clear the filters that are keeping the answers foggy and dim. Sharpen your intuition and spiritual gifts of knowing and discerning. As you do this, the Holy Spirit will plug you in to your answers and turn the light switches on to your truth. You will never be led astray by your own personal guidance system. As you choose to make God's will your will, you are guaranteed success and your compass will bring you home God will be able to congratulate you on the successful outcomes you have experienced as the creator of your life. He will say to you, "Well done, thou good and faithful servant: thou hast been faithful over a few things, I will make thee ruler over many things."[23]

---

[23] Matthew 25:20.

Everyone in Your Life Plays a Part in Your Play, with a Script You Have Given Them

If you are the creator of your life, then you have created everyone that is now in your life or has been in your life, to play a role for you. Imagine your life as a play, a drama you have created in order to facilitate the lessons you have come to earth to learn. William Shakespeare said it well with these words, "All the world is a stage, and all the men and women in it merely players. They have their exits and entrances, and one man in his time plays many parts."

We need people to have parts in our play and play out certain roles for us so that we can learn what we came to learn. Wake up from the drama, and move closer to spiritual mastery.

We gave each of the people in our life drama a script to follow, to assist us in our learning. Every time we hold others in blame, anger, and resentment, we have forgotten we gave them a script and are not learning the lesson they offer us. When someone moves out of your play, it may be because you either learned or refused to learn the lesson. If we have not learned the lesson, we will attract someone else to play that part, usually in a more magnified way for us. We get to keep playing out the drama until the learning occurs. When the lesson is learned, we are free to create a new drama with new people. Just as we have people to play the roles for us in our drama, many times we play a role in others' dramas.

We live at a time where we are meant to wake up to our God-selves. We created our dramas and the people in them so that we would pay attention and respond to them. As humans we tend to be conditioned to doing the same thing over and over. We knew we would be living on the earth at a time when we would become conditioned by our roles in life. We knew that going to work and making money would occupy a lot of our time and attention. We needed dramas that would literally "knock us off our feet" so we would notice that there are imbalances at the deepest levels of our being.

We came here to awaken our god-self within us and integrate into our consciousness the characteristics of Christ inherent in us. In order to truly become unconditionally loving, compassionate, and forgiving, we would need people in our play that would hurt us, offend us, and use us. We need people to be poor and needy. We need people to become sick and even die. Without their participation we would only know the concept of Christ-like characteristics without the physical expression of them. We need people to play all the parts so that we can choose to respond in a Christ-like manner and claim and master these attributes as part of who we are. Many people say they aspire to know their Christ-self and yet when the perfect drama occurs in their lives—to give them the opportunity to choose the expression of Christ-like characteristics—they often feel it is more than they have the capacity to offer or should have to offer. In an awakened state of Christ-consciousness, we are able to appreciate all the life experiences we have had and feel immense gratitude for all the people who have played their parts for us.

I have worked with many clients that came to me to clear the residual energy of powerlessness and deeper beliefs of worth- lessness created by their experience of having been abused as a child. In most cases, their anger, resentment, and blame for their victim status in life is due to the hurt brought upon them as a child. They say to me, "Why would I have created this? A child would not choose to be sexually abused."

I explain to them that I believe that as a child they did not make a conscious choice to be abused. The choice was probably made in the spirit realm before they came to earth. They may have agreed to a childhood experience of abuse for a variety of reasons. Maybe they were the one appointed to break the abuse pattern in their generations. Maybe through their experience they would alter the energy of abuse by clearing it and taking on roles in their adult life to influence more safety for children. Maybe it was the perfect experience for them to truly come to know the capacity they have for unconditional love and forgiveness. The experience of childhood sexual abuse could cause them to turn within, to the deepest parts of their being, to discover and awaken their Christ-like compassion. At whatever level we have known pain, anger, and resent- ment, it is to that same level and beyond that we can experience joy, love, and peace.

Compassion is not something you have to figure out or intellectually force. The characteristic of Christ-like compassion is natural and already exists within us. As you set an intention to awaken the energy of compassion within you, the grace of God imbues you and it happens.

⌒

    Jill had been sexually abused as a child. She carried tremendous hate, anger, and blame towards her father for the abuse she suffered from him and felt it was his fault that her life was so riddled with pain and struggle. She had refused to have any relationship with him for the past several years. She wondered if she would ever have the ability or even the desire to reconcile with him. He was elderly and was experiencing an illness that might soon end his physical life. This troubled her because she worried that if he died, she wasn't even sure she would be able to attend his funeral. She had made the decision to no longer hide her true feelings and was not going to go if she still felt so negatively toward him.

    After a few sessions, she came in one day and said a miracle had occurred. She shared that she no longer held any ill feelings toward her father. She had contacted him earlier in the week and apologized to him for causing any pain in his life. She told him she would like to have a relationship with him free of any reference to the past and would like to start anew.

    She told me she understood that clearing all the old energies had allowed her to start feeling and perceiving her trauma in a whole new light. One night she had offered a very powerful prayer, asking her

God to help her to move forward and learn what this experience had been designed to teach her.

That night she had a dream, wherein she saw herself and her father in the Heavens as spirits before they were born. As a spirit, she had asked her father to play this role for her. She knew she wanted to make a difference and help her family heal from generational patterns of abuse; therefore, she would require someone in her family to help once again create the abuse, so it could be cleared and the energy of forgiveness and compassion would be awakened and released to be received by herself, her ancestors, and posterity. Her father resisted and did not want to play this role for her. She pleaded with him to do this. He told her he would do it on one condition, that she would never stop loving him.

As Jill recalled this dream to me, we both wept as we felt the Holy Spirit manifest the truth of this spiritual recollection in her life. She said that the next day she felt that the residual negative energy from the abuse had been lifted off her and had been replaced by a genuine deep feeling of love and gratitude for her father.

Within the year her father did pass on. She not only attended the funeral, but she spoke a eulogy expressing her great love and appreciation for the many great things that he had taught her. Many of the people in the congregation knew there had been family disagreements and problems, but did not know the details. They only knew that Jill and her father had not spoken for many years. That day they were able to witness the capacity we each have for compassion, unconditional love, and forgiveness. Jill offered everyone in attendance the opportunity to look at his or her own life and choose the same. She is a great example and her story bears witness to how quickly healing can occur when we have the faith to manifest it.

~~~

Jill would agree that her father played a very big role in her play. She has shared with me how grateful she is that she awoke to this knowing so she could free him from his role before he died and she was able to create a new experience with him.

So, has everyone who plays a "bad guy" role chosen to do so on our behalf? In many instances I believe this is true. I also believe there are some people just choosing to be bad. These individuals have come into this state of freedom and choice and have decided to be agents of destruction instead of construction. In either case, we have the power to attract them into our lives to play a role for us, and we also have the power to release them. We have the power to prevent attracting these people into our lives by choosing to attract safe and loving people. We can prevent experiences of being hurt and violated by others by keeping our attention on what we want.

Since Everyone in Your Life
Plays a Part in Your Play
—with a Script You Have Given Them—
You Can Change the Scripts Any Time

If you have handed out the scripts to the people in your life, and there are some you don't like, change the scripts. Your creative powers and abilities of thought and feeling have the power to influence the changing or leaving of the people in your life. If you are willing to imagine the people that you perceive as treating you poorly as people who treat you well, you will cause this change to occur.

Many clients say to me, "I can't imagine that person being nice to me, they have always been that way." I will say to them "What part of you is still believing you deserve to be treated poorly? The only reason it is showing up in your life is because at some level you are believing that is how you deserve to be treated and you keep attracting it!"

I take them through the following visualization process to assist this change:

Imagine your life as a play. You are standing on a stage with all the people in your life standing on the stage with you. Thank everyone for showing up and helping you learn your life lessons. Express gratitude for everyone playing out his or her parts so well. You can even go around the stage and thank each person individually for the lesson they have helped you learn.

Once you have expressed your gratitude, invite all those who have played a part with a negative script to come forward. All those with a negative script are asked to throw these demeaning scripts into a big bonfire. If they are unwilling, they are escorted off the stage by stagehands to create their negative script with someone else.

After the old scripts are gone, Christ is there to hand out new scripts to everyone, including a new script for you. All the new scripts direct everyone to love and honor you and your new script is to receive this love and honor because you now love and honor yourself. Imagine everyone reading through their scripts, getting familiar with the details. Point out to anyone individual details that you would like them to notice so that you can make sure they are aware of the changes in their behavior towards you. Thank everyone for his or her willingness to play off a new script. They all are happy to because they know this is your play and they want to show up how you have asked them to. Have everyone start acting out his or her new parts with you and notice in detail the new healthy behavior you are experiencing in your play. Know at any time that you can stop your play and change the scripts as many times as you want. Always see the people in your play as agreeable and willing to take a new script. If they are not willing to take the new script, have them escorted off your stage.

In the motion picture *Titanic,* you may recall the closing scene. In this scene, Rose has died and gone to the spirit realm and is once again a young woman. She is walking up the grand staircase of the ship, and Jack, her true love, is waiting for her at the top with his hand outstretched. The camera pans the balcony above the staircase showing everyone who played a character in the movie, applauding her. All the people who loved her and supported her, and the people who played the bad guys for her, are all present and applauding her successful life. I find it interesting that everyone is there, at the conclusion of her life, as she is being reunited with her true love. Everyone is present to honor her.

The spiritual higher self of everyone in your life really loves and honors you. The main reason you are not experiencing this with everyone in your life is because you still believe you need people to play those negative parts for you.

Release all the bad guys in your play to become good guys. You no longer have to keep playing out the drama of hurting, judging, and controlling one another.

As each of us awakens our Christ-consciousness, we will draw that same energy out of others in all our interactions with them. Be willing to stand in your true power and light. Know that when you do, you give others unspoken permission and support to choose the same. Set an intention to bring out the best in everyone you interact with. Say to yourself, *I am attracting people into my life who respect and honor me, and I respect and honor them. My Christ-energy brings out the best in all those I meet and interact with. I am grateful for the comfortable and delicious interactions I have daily with all the like-minded people who are in my life.*

CHAPTER

45

*H*OW TO KEEP YOURSELF STUCK

We are in a new energy of healing. It is about remembering who we really are. Many of the processes that were once effective are now keeping people stuck. Talk therapy and support groups can be two such practices. If you are involved in either of these, and the focus of your time in them is on the past and what happened to you, you are stuck. You are putting your attention on what you don't want—which just creates more of it in your life.

Many of the people who play parts for you in your current life may be different from those in your childhood. Most likely, many of these same patterns of your childhood are still present in your current life. As the planet Earth continues to ascend and move into its glorified status, the planet's magnetic fields are dropping and the earth's frequency is rising. The effect this has on us is that we get to experience everything with more magnitude and intensity. It is the planet's agreement with us that helps us get unstuck. Whatever pushes your buttons will be very potent for you, so you will notice it and change it.

If you need your support group to validate you, you still believe you are not enough. It is time to validate yourself and be honest with yourself. If you believe you are anything less than wonderful, powerful, appreciated, and honored, then you are believing a lie. Ask God to reveal to you through the Holy Spirit what is keeping you stuck. Step into the new energy of healing and see how quickly your life can change for the better.

If you like support, either one-on-one or in groups, find people who are focused on creating rather than recovering. There is a movement toward the spiritual being part of psychotherapy. Personally, I wouldn't engage someone as my support person if they ignored or left out spiritual aspects. That's what this has all been about: bringing our spiritual self and our physical self into one body.

Pay attention to what is keeping you stuck. If you are still engaged in the same processes, with very little change in your life, notice that it's probably not working any more. Demand results from the people you pay to assist you in making some quantum leaps to a clearer and happier state of being.

If you find it hard to move on, then you are still looking for recognition as a victim. If you still need to tell your story of a childhood from hell, then you need your story to validate how much you've been through. So, your life was hard. Great. You did a great job of designing it. So, the people were really mean and evil. Great. They played their parts really well.

Wouldn't it be nice if instead of sharing our stories so we can be recognized for the pain we've lived through, we would no longer see it as pain? Its just energy. In the sharing, honor each other for the creative dramas we each designed and for how much fun we've all had in the experience of learning and remembering who we really are through them.

It's About Healing Marriages, Not Breaking them Up

I have had many clients say to me during their first session, "I don't see how I can stay married to my spouse." They can't even imagine their life getting any better with the person for whom they once felt only love and admiration. I once heard someone say, "We date and date and date, until we meet the person who pushes our buttons bigger than anyone else, and then we marry them!" I believe this is true. The person we choose to marry is someone we have attracted into our lives to help us become aware of our deeper issues. They become one of our biggest mirrors. We have the potential to create some of our greatest pain with this person, and we also have the potential to create some of our greatest joy. If you focus on blame and resentment toward your spouse, you are on the pain side. You will get to joy faster when your spouse shows negativity toward you, and you are able to say to yourself, *Why did I create this? What part of me still believes I don't deserve love and respect?* You may come from a long line of broken marriages and families, and you have the stewardship to clear this pattern for yourself, your ancestors, and your posterity.

I believe every marriage and family has a blueprint for success in the matrix of its energy. What is required to have a successful and happy marriage and family is for all participants to take responsibility and to be accountable for their creations. As each person chooses to be accountable for clearing their negative energies and beliefs, he or she is free to create healthy relationship patterns. If you don't clear and change with the person who is currently pushing your buttons, you will end up creating the same disharmonies with someone else. If you have children, it is better to clear out your baggage and to work out your issues with the other parent of your children than to leave that person and break up your children's family.

Divorce is a pattern that wants to be cleared from our culture. It is complete in the lessons it has offered us. Choose to heal your marriage so your family can stay intact. Clients will ask me, "What if my spouse doesn't want to do this? What if they don't want to change?" I then ask them if they believe their spouse can change and if they can imagine their spouse the way they desire them to be. I tell them that if they can't, their spouse will never be anything but who they are now.

You have co-created the current state of your marriage. The next time you are starting to get at each other, stop yourself. Say to your spouse, "I love you and respect you. I don't want to do this anymore. I want to create a loving and honoring relationship with you. What do you want?"

If your spouse is cold to you, they have inner-child states existing subconsciously within them that are wounded. Any time you are in a conflict in a marriage, you both are in the energy of a wounded inner-child. All you can do at this point is protect yourself from getting hurt again.

Clear and heal your inner-child wounds. As you clear and are restored to the true essence of your self, you will be free to show up and stay in your adult energy. In this energy, you are able to receive inspiration on behalf of your marriage to help facilitate it shifting into a healthy momentum. If your heart or your spouse's heart has turned cold, ask God to soften it. Thank him for softening your heart and your spouse's.

I have experienced that those same clients who believed their marriage was beyond repair said to me after a few sessions that their spouse was changing, without even being in therapy. What happens is that as one person clears, everyone they are closely networked with gets a piece of that clearing. As their vibration rises, the vibration of the people closest to them rises also. As they imagine their spouse playing off a new script of love and honor, they invite and influence that behavior coming from their spouse.

Sometimes there are hidden values attached to your spouse not changing. In Patricia's case, if her husband changed to be loving and kind to her instead of verbally abusive and controlling, she wouldn't have anything to share with her friends to gain sympathy. In her sessions, she said she wanted her husband to change and also discovered she was reluctant to have this happen. Subconsciously she still believed that the only attention she would get was through her friends feeling sorry for her. With this belief, she needed her husband to continue to play the mean, nasty husband part, so she could continue to go to lunch with her girlfriends and tell them the latest nasty things he had said or done. They always responded sympathetically and supported her. This experience helped counter the deeper belief that her real self was unlovable and unimportant to others. She was reluctant to change this pattern for fear that if she had no stories to tell, the friends she cared about would fade out of her life.

With this awareness she was able to clear her core issues and put her attention on her husband showing up loving and kind. Her attention to this allowed energy to flow to it, and helped awaken those behaviors in her husband. She was no longer triggered into the old energy of her wounded child when he showed up in his negative patterns. Staying in her clear adult energy allowed her to communicate in a loving and respectful manner, speaking the words of inspiration that came to her to help them both create a healthier marriage.

Creating healthy marriages creates healthy families. I have been married to my first and only husband for more than twenty years. We have four wonderful children. I speak from experience when it comes to what I believe it takes to keep a marriage thriving. If you give your marriage no attention, you will hardly have a marriage. If you give your marriage mediocre attention, you will have a mediocre marriage. If you make it a priority and give it regular, positive attention, it will thrive. To support your marriage thriving, try doing all or some of the following:

1. Pray together as a couple out loud, each taking turns, at least once a day.

2. Praise your spouse with all the wonderful things you wish they would say to you.

3. Create a new script for them by writing in detail what you believe your ideal companion would be like. Live by that script yourself.

4. Ask each other what one thing you say or do that hurts them deeply. Choose never to say or do it again.

5. Create "What We Want More of" lists. Ask the Heavens to help you create them.

6. Stop talking about what's not working or what you don't want. Start talking about what's working and what you want more of.

7. Choose to say only positive things to others about your spouse.

8. If you find you create conflict at the same time or place in your home, start clearing the patterns by noticing it and stopping it. For example, if you always fight about money in the evening in the bedroom, agree not to recreate that again. Talk about money Saturday morning as you go for a walk together. Set an intention. It will be a harmonious, successful experience.

9. Have sex a lot because you enjoy it.

10. Play together often. Go on a date night alone once a week.

11. Take a trip for just the two of you once a year.

Many people who have been married several years begin to take their marriage and their spouse for granted. Bad habits and lazy attitudes that would have never been acted out in their courtship days have taken over. How fresh and vital is your marriage? How much respect, tenderness, and unconditional love do you exemplify towards your spouse daily? Marriage is a sacred relationship that demands constant attention on our part in order to thrive. Marriage is our modern-day temple that we enter into to bring up all of our issues so we can be purified and return to a state of wholeness. Add to the beauty and reverence of your marriage by treating yourself and your spouse like a god that you humbly revere and adore, because that is who you both truly are. Sanctify your marriage with God's help and it can be one of your greatest treasures on earth.

*T*EN LIES WE THINK ARE LOVE

Real love is an energy that supports us in feeling good. When we feel genuine self-love and self-worth we experience ourselves as good enough and capable. There is a reverence and humility that accompanies this deep knowledge that we are valuable just for being our unique selves. Our worth is not dependent on our doings or our belongings. When genuine self-love and self-worth are present and alive within us, we attract love and respect from others. We literally draw to us the energy of love from others. We offer the energy of love and receive the energy of love. We feel very whole and complete in this state of being.

When we are born, we are completely dependent on others for our survival both physically and emotionally. Most of us grew up with our physical needs being met adequately and emotional needs being met sporadically or not at all.

We come into this world with the need to be validated that we are loveable. We are looking for someone—primarily our parents—to tell us that we are important, we are loved and cherished, and that we count, free of any conditions. Even though our spirit knows we are loveable, our cognitive physical self needs to hear that. We need to be validated through our infancy, childhood, and teen years as we move through different developmental stages. If we were not given that message and our environment caused us to feel threatened or unsafe, we are still looking to have the message that we are loveable given to us as adults. We are stuck in patterns of co-dependency: looking for love and validation outside of ourselves.

When we were little and love was not as available or predictable, we learned to live without it. We subconsciously created ways of thinking and behaving that helped us feel safer in what seemed like a random world.

You may have tried different ways to get more love and support to feel more loveable. Some of those ways worked and you did get more attention. When these patterns didn't work, you adapted to limiting beliefs held at a deep, subconscious level that tell you that you are really not loveable. We often sabotage the experience we want the most because it is so unfamiliar, and at that deep level we really believe we don't deserve it, that we are not worth it, or that the love is not real.

The Ten Lies We Think Are Love

1. *Food is love*

    Our bodies require love through appropriate touch. When that need has not been met, we often turn to food to fill us. The root cause of all addictions is the body's need for attention. Food feels good to the body. The body will begin to believe food is love and continually seek it out to get the feeling of sweetness and fullness that the energy of real love gives us when it is open and flowing in our being.

2. *Sex is love*

   This can play out in a way that supports people in fearing, hating, and despising sex or becoming addicted to it. If you were sexually abused or prematurely affected by sexual experiences, it is common to have the deeper belief of, *I can only be loved for sex.* Sexual encounters can feel abusive and leave you with a feeling of being used. Sexual addictions are supported by the body's need for affection. Again, the body needs touch and support. If you were sexually abused as a child or that pattern is still alive from generations past, your body may hold the belief, *My body is bad because it feels good.* It goes through a cycle of feeling starved for love, getting a quick fix with sex, and then feeling bad for satisfying its need for love with sex.

3. *Money is love*

   This pattern can get set up in families with money. When emotional love does not flow freely, money is often used as a substitute. This can set up siblings as rivals because they subconsciously know that there is not enough emotional love to go around and they must vie for mom and dad's money and possessions. Mom and dad's money and possessions represent the energy of real love that they have never had. As adults, money represents security. Security supports us in feeling safe. This can also feel like love. The more money you have, the more safe you feel, and the more loved you feel.

4. *I have to be sick or ill to be loved*

   If you were given more attention when you were sick or

ill as a child, you may still believe that you need this pattern to get noticed. If you were healthy and well, you would risk no one caring about you. Doctors can act as surrogate parents. They give you attention, advice, and hopefully encouragement—all the things you needed as a child. Your sickness may be a way to keep you from living your life fully or taking responsibility for your life because you feel incapable and afraid. It is something to fall back on when you need to escape and want to hide.

5. *I have to suffer to get love*

People in abusive relationships create this pattern and are not familiar with healthy love and how it operates in a relationship. If you were beaten, slapped, hit, and physically punished in your childhood, or that pattern has been in your family, you may believe that love is being hurt. You may even sabotage healthy relationships so you can feel your familiar experience once again.

6. *I have to fix people to be loved*

Many people have a deeper belief that if they are not helping people get better they have no value. If they have no value, they cannot be loveable. The problem with this pattern is that if you need to fix sick and dysfunctional people in order to feel loveable, you will continually attract these people into your life and they will not get well. You need them to be "unfixable" so you can stay "loveable."

7. *I have to control you to make it safe to let you love me*

Control is one of the biggest patterns in relationships. The deeper belief is, *I will control you before you control me.* It is common for two controllers to be together in a relationship with each only seeing the other in a controlling pattern. I have worked with numerous couples where both are controllers. I will ask them separately, "Who do you believe controls the relationship?" They will always say that the other person does. Blame is a big part of the controller's experience. Victim energy is at the root of the pattern. At a deeper level, if you still believe you are a victim, you may use control to create a feeling of safety to prevent yourself from ever being a victim again.

8. *I have to please others to be loved*

    This pattern is often the opposite of a controller pattern. It is more common for women to play this role in a relationship with a controlling man. In this pattern, the person is always thinking of other people before thinking of him or herself. Everything is processed with the underlying thought, *What will others think? What do others want? What do I have to do or say to make sure they are happy?* Chronic fatigue and other energy depletion disorders are common with this pattern.

9. *If I let you love me, you will leave me*

    Abandonment is at the core of this pattern. If you were abandoned as a child, you may fear that the people you love will get hurt, die, or go away. In order to prevent this from happening, you will not let a relationship go very far or you will sabotage it. It is common to hold the deeper belief—*I'll abandon you before you abandon me*—because you still believe that since every relationship ends in abandonment, you might as well be in control of it. That way it doesn't hurt as much and it is more predictable.

10. *Love hurts; relationships are painful*

This belief will only support you in creating unhealthy, painful relationships. You will continue to attract people who create a lot of pain. You will support your relationships in being painful in the way you perceive them, think about them, and the choices you make in them. You will go from one relationship to another feeling victimized and hurt and wondering when real love will come your way, or you will believe you're stuck in a relationship that can never work and you will never be happy.

The first step to healing these patterns is to understand that your beliefs create your experience. Whatever you believe, both subconsciously and consciously is what you are getting in life. If you don't like what you are getting, change your beliefs. Many of these beliefs are at a subconscious level and are generational beliefs. That means that we come from a long line of people who have carried the belief and have created the experience that matches it. Limiting beliefs are also rooted in our childhood experiences. You have the opportunity to take control of the phenomenal power of your mind to release these old beliefs and create new ones. If you are really stuck, I recommend a tool like RET that releases the energy that supports these old beliefs and patterns staying in place.

Look at your relationships and notice what you keep experiencing. What keeps getting recreated in your life? This will tell you a lot about what relationship beliefs you hold. Change your relationships by changing your beliefs.

Everyone carries limiting beliefs and patterns that they came to clear. In clearing these energies, we heal the lies that we thought were truths about ourselves. We thought they were true because we kept having experiences that made us think, *This keeps happening to me so it must be true!* As you change your beliefs, you change your life, and understand now that you can create whatever you want.

I believe that God set in place within each of us the real energy of love. It is a powerful energy just waiting to be awakened. Another person cannot awaken it. Only you hold the key to the energy of real love inside of you. As you open and honor this energy by loving yourself, forgiving yourself, and being kind and patient with yourself, you are then free to receive the real love others have to offer you. If you are a controller and/or a blamer, the first step for you is to take accountability for your life and own your life's creation.

No one can create your life but you. God wants to co-create a life of joy, wellness, and prosperity with you. He cannot do it for you, only with you. Choose now to create healthy, loving, honest relationships that add value to your life. Be willing to end any relationships that cannot be healthy. Hold as your motto or mantra:

I am worthy of real love. I deserve to be loved and admired by a healthy, loving person. I am attracting people that can and want to create healthy, loving relationships with me. I am ending relationships that cannot be healthy. God loves me, and I love myself.

It's about Healing Families, Not Breaking Them Up

Families have been through a lot these last few decades. How is your family doing? Look at your families: the one you grew up in as a child and the one you have created as an adult. Are you at peace, and are you reconciled with your parents and siblings? Or are you holding back because of the way they treat you now, or what they did to you in the past? If you are estranged from or embittered toward any of these family members, you have some things to remedy. Look at your adult family members: your current spouse, ex-spouses, sons, and daughters. How are those relationships?

Healing your extended family relationships does not mean you have to hang out with these people and spend a lot of time with them. The bottom line is that you may not have a lot in common or enjoy the same interests. Healing means feeling clear of any negative emotion towards them, being able to feel a sustaining peace that keeps you free of any expectations of them, knowing about their lives and loving them regardless, and allowing them, free of any judgment, what they are choosing to create.

If you perceive your extended family members in a negative light, you project that energy onto them, and they easily and willingly show themselves to you that way to make you right. Everyone in your family is playing a role for you. They each have a script that you have given them, and they are just actors on your stage playing out the part you have asked them to play. Wake up to who you really are, see them for who they really are, and release them from these old energy scripts. In your mind, be willing to start seeing them play a new role for you—one of honor, love, respect, and enjoyment.

If you are a parent, you have a great responsibility to your children. You have a stewardship in their lives to love and support them. No matter their age—from infancy to adulthood—you agreed as a spirit to give them this love and support as their parent. If you have hurt them, make amends. Be accountable for your actions and nurture a healthy relationship. Do not make your children be substitute parents for you. I have worked with many clients who abandoned their own needs as children to try to make their mom or dad happy. They play this role out into their adult life until they can't do it any more. They begin to resent mom and dad and then subconsciously believe that the only way to get out is to abandon their parents.

Tim was a classic case of making his mom's needs more important than his own as a child. His birth was very rough on his mother, which left an imprint in his subconscious mind of, *I hurt women*. His mom was very depressed and his dad was emotionally checked-out and physically absent. At the tender age of two, Tim made a subconscious decision to try to make his mom happy. He tried energetically to fill in for his father not being there. He didn't want to lose his mom, too. In his sessions, the two-year-old subconscious part of Tim cleared deeper beliefs like:

- ❖ Mom's needs are more important than mine.
- ❖ I don't have any needs; there is nothing I really need.
- ❖ It's not really love if I ask for it.
- ❖ I feel afraid to ask for love because I probably won't get it.
- ❖ Commitment equals feeling trapped.
- ❖ I make Mom unhappy.
- ❖ Where's Dad? He's never here.
- ❖ Adult men abandon women.
- ❖ Women are controlling and keep men trapped.
- ❖ I can't stay; I have to get away.

Through guided imagery, Tim easily brought his little two-year-old self into the light with Christ. We asked the two-year-old self what his job was. He said, "To try to make Mom happy." I asked him how successful he had been. He said, "Not very successful." I then had his adult self, while they were in the light, tell him that he didn't have to do this job any more, that he was only two, and to give the job to Jesus and his angels. At this point he saw his mom in the light being assisted by

her guardian angels who were loving her and taking care of her. After the guided imagery, we filled
the two-year-old Tim with the following new
beliefs:

❖ We love you and are there for you.

❖ There is nothing you have to do to be loved.

❖ All your needs are important to us.

❖ You can ask for whatever you want.

To assist Tim in his current role we focused on these
new beliefs:

❖ I am loved.

❖ I am important.

❖ I am experiencing commitment as freeing and
honoring.

❖ I am a loving, supportive, available father.

❖ I am creating a harmonious relationship with the
mother of my children.

❖ I am attracting women who are pleasant
and happy.

This pattern of believing he had to take care of adult
women followed Tim into his adult life. He attracted a
woman who, soon into their marriage, became very
unhappy and depressed all the time. She held a deeper
belief that husbands abandon their wives. Their two
patterns drove them to divorce after they had many years
of marriage and six children. I believe they could have
prevented the divorce if they both had cleared their core

issues and had learned new life skills for creating a healthy marriage and family.

The children of this couple are the ones that lose the most. Most likely one or more of them will step into the role of the parent that left in their relationship with the parent with whom they spend most of their time. The generational patterns of dysfunction carry on, growing stronger and more destructive with each new generation.

The interesting thing about Tim's life was that getting out of his marriage did not clear his deeper beliefs about his role with women, so he kept attracting more women with the same patterns. As a result of his sessions with me, he became aware of and cleared these deeper belief patterns and started attracting what he really wanted: a harmonious relationship with his former wife; close, loving, honest, supportive relationships with each of his children; and sometime in the future, a healthy, loving, spiritual partnership with a happy woman.

If your family is struggling, divorce is not the remedy. Do all that you can to turn the momentum around. Clear your wounded child issues and co-dependent patterns, and learn new, healthy life skills. Your family is your greatest gift from God. Treat it as such. Be a great parent. Be a loving, kind, easy-to-live-with spouse. As a parent, show up for your children to instruct, guide, and lead them. Allow your children their experiences as they choose to create their lives. Trust that the cause and effect of the Law of Attraction will give them the consequences and the learning they need.

I pray for my four children daily. I express prayers like this regularly:

Dear God, thank you for watching over my children and keeping them safe. Thank you for helping me see their higher selves. I pray that as they make choices that are disharmonious to their core desires, the results of these choices will return to them magnified and they will know and feel discomfort if it is not what they want. As they make choices that are harmonious with their core desires, the results will be magnified, and they will notice and feel tremendous peace. Thank you for helping me be sensitive to their needs. Fill me with inspiration to know what to say and when to say it, so they will know their great worth. Thank you for reminding me to hug them and to look them in the eyes when we are interacting. Thank you for orchestrating more opportunities that will create more feelings of love, trust, honor, and playfulness between us. I love playing with my children. Thank you for all the grand adventures we have had and for the many more that are coming. Thank you, God, for watching over and sending ministering angels to their future spouses to help prepare them for my children so they can come together and create joyful families. In the name of Jesus Christ, amen.

Along with daily prayers like this one, the following are a few ideas to help strengthen your family:

1. Pray together as a family once each day. In our family of six people, we each take a day of the week to say all the prayers for that day: family prayer, prayer at meals, and

any other prayers. "Whose day is it to pray?" is heard often at our house.

2. Eat together at a sit-down meal at least four times a week. More often is even better.

3. Tell each of your children individually, "If there is any thing I say or do that makes you feel worthless or not good enough, stop me and tell me. I love you and want to treat you with respect and honor."

4. Have a family activity once a week: anything—cleaning up the yard, going to the movies, reading a book together, watching old family videos, or doing something for someone else.

5. Let your children witness often how much you love and respect their mom or dad.

6. When one of your children comes to you dissatisfied with their current life experience, rather than sympathizing with them and talking about what they don't want, which will only help them create more of it, say to them, "Why are you creating this? If you could have it the way you want it, what would that look like?" Help them become aware that they, with God, are the creators of their lives.

7. Take car trips together where everybody is together a lot!

8. Most of the time when you vacation, go only with your family so that your children are focused on each other and their friendships can grow.

9. Never use demeaning or derogatory language or voice tones with each other. Hostile humor is saying something negative in a funny way. It is really

shame with laughter. If someone is using a negative
voice tone, politely say, "Please change your tone."
10. Hug your children every day. Better yet, tuck them in
bed, no matter what age they are.

Your family is your greatest stewardship. A modern-day
prophet, David O. McKay, said, "Nothing can compensate for
failure in the home." Your most vital and sacred agreements are
with your family. Many times in your life your family members
will play roles for you to support you in learning your biggest lessons. How do you currently perceive your family? Are they your
greatest gift or your greatest pain and hardship? Banish pride and
ego from your stature. Be humble and submissive in your familial
role. In this state, you invite God to take you by the hand and
lead you to success in this most sacred stewardship.

MESSAGES YOUR CHILDREN NEED TO HEAR

The best parenting class I have ever taken was my own healing. Becoming aware of all the unmet needs that I carried subconsciously and consciously as a "wounded inner-child," provided for me the awareness of what my children needed from me. What I wanted and needed to hear and receive as a child is what my children want and need.

Helping many people clear their childhood wounds and reparent their inner child with the help of God's love and grace has taught me how to be a better parent.

There are a series of developmental stages we go through in our childhood. John Bradshaw does an excellent job of reviewing them in his book, *Homecoming: Reclaiming and Championing Your Inner Child*. Reading this book years ago in an effort to heal my own inner child has turned into the best parenting experience I have ever had.

As parents we have a sacred stewardship to provide for our children's physical, emotional, mental, and spiritual developmental needs. Children come into the world needing their parents to affirm and validate their worth. When this does not happen, they grow into adults who create co-dependent relationships in an effort to make others affirm and validate them.

If you are one of those adults still giving power to others to tell you, "You are worthwhile," take back the power and become your own healthy parent. Give the job to Heavenly Mother and Father to flow to you the energy of a parent's love to validate your great worth. Heavenly Mother and Father are your first and original parents. Release your earthly parents and all other adults from this job. Through God's magnificent grace you can have all your needs met as if you came from an ideal childhood.

As a parent, use the following affirmations with your own children to send them messages of validation during the different stages of their growing years. If your children have grown out of some of these stages, it is still not too late. Our child energies are always a part of us. Even if you have adult children, ask the angels to manifest opportunities for you to speak these messages to your children. They will feel the love you have for them as their parent and greater love will be shared between you.

Infancy (birth – nine months old)

Developmental need: To be validated for "being who you are."

- ❖ Welcome to the world, we've been eagerly waiting for you.
- ❖ We have prepared a special place for you.
- ❖ All your needs are important to us. We will provide for you willingly.

❖ You can be touched and held when you want to.

❖ You are more important than any of my doings.

❖ We love you just the way you are.

❖ There is nothing you have to "do" to be loved.

❖ We like feeding you, bathing you, changing you, and spending time with you.

❖ We want to take care of you and are prepared to do that.

❖ You are a gift to the world. In all the world there has never been another like you.

❖ God smiled the day you were born.

Toddler (nine – eighteen months old)

Developmental need: Supported in exploring, sensing, and doing in the world.

❖ It's okay to be curious, to want, to look, to touch, and to taste things.

❖ We will make it safe for you to explore.

❖ We love you just the way you are.

❖ We are here to take care of your needs. You do not have to take care of ours.

❖ It is okay for you to be taken care of.

❖ It is okay for you to say no.

❖ It is okay for us to be different. We will work out our differences.

❖ It's okay to feel your emotions.

❖ Your emotions are important to us.

❖ You can be you, and we will always love you.

❖ We love watching you grow and learn to walk and talk, and start separating from us.

❖ We love and value you.

Preschooler (three – six years old)

Developmental need: Coming into your own identity and power.

❖ It is okay for you to test your boundaries and find out your limits.

❖ We will set appropriate limits for you to keep you safe and help you find out who you are.

❖ We like your energy; we like your curiosity about life.

❖ It's okay for you to think for yourself, and we will think for ourselves.

❖ You can think about your feelings and have feelings about what you are thinking.

❖ You can know what you need and ask for help.

❖ It's okay for you to feel any way you want to feel.

❖ We see and appreciate your wholeness.

❖ You can think and feel at the same time.

❖ We are glad you are starting to think for yourself.

❖ You can try out different ways of using your power.

❖ We love to listen to you.

❖ We are here for you.

❖ We love to do things with you.

❖ It's okay to cry even though you are growing up.

❖ It is good for you to find out the cause and effect of your behavior.

- ❖ You can ask questions if something confuses you.
- ❖ You are not responsible for our marriage.
- ❖ You are not responsible for our happiness.
- ❖ You are not responsible for the problems in our family.
- ❖ It's okay for you to explore who you are.

School–Age (six – twelve years old)

Developmental need: Fitting in, having structure, knowing, and learning.

- ❖ You can be your own unique self at school.
- ❖ There is no one you have to please.
- ❖ It's okay to learn to do things your own way.
- ❖ It's okay to think about things and try them out before you make them your own.
- ❖ You can trust your own judgments
- ❖ You can do things your own way, and it's okay to disagree.
- ❖ We love you just the way you are.
- ❖ You can trust your feelings to guide you and to know what you want.
- ❖ It is okay to want. You can have dreams and desires.
- ❖ You deserve to have the things you want. It will be fun to see how they show up.
- ❖ You can ask your angels to help you manifest what you want.
- ❖ You have a lot of spiritual help to assist you in creating what you want in life.

- ❖ You can dress the way other kids dress, or you can dress your own way.
- ❖ We respect and trust your choice of friends.
- ❖ We love growing with you.
- ❖ God is watching over you and cares very deeply for you.
- ❖ The world is a safe place; there is so much goodness for you to experience.
- ❖ You deserve to attract safe and loving people into your life.

Adolescence (thirteen – eighteen years old)

Developmental need: Separating and creating independence from family.

- ❖ You can take all the time you need to grow up.
- ❖ You can know who you are and learn and practice skills for independence.
- ❖ You can grow in your maleness and femaleness.
- ❖ You can still feel dependent at times.
- ❖ We are happy with your choices.
- ❖ Our love is always with you.
- ❖ It is okay to make mistakes.
- ❖ You can always choose again.
- ❖ We trust you to ask for help.
- ❖ We look forward to knowing you as an adult.
- ❖ You can develop your own interests, relationships, and causes.
- ❖ You can learn about sex and nurturing, and be

responsible for your needs, feelings, and behaviors.

❖ We approve of you.

❖ We love you.

Affirm your children often with these validating phrases. Affirm your own inner child to finally receive love, respect, and support. Fulfill your sacred obligation of being the safest, kindest, most loving, affirming parent you can be. You cannot give a child too much validation. God created us to be loved and validated. Make a choice to stop passing down the wounds of your family to your children, by being the best parent you can be. Raise your child using these phrases and others that the Holy Spirit gives you so your children are free to grow into their adult experience knowing themselves as God knows them. In this knowing, they will carry with them a reverence and humility for being anchored in their truth.

Your Spirit Is Whole and Complete

Your spirit is always whole, but everyone's spirit is at a different light vibration. Your spirit is energy patterns of sound and light that is being focused on your physical reality as its primary focal point. As you come into mortality, your spirit is fragmented into different points of attraction influenced both by your DNA and by generational patterns and beliefs. You essentially start this experience fragmented and split. Your spirit is still intact: it just took on negative energies. You are like a pure glass of water that had some sand and grit poured into it. The sand and grit settled to the bottom and your challenging life experiences are like having the glass shaken up. You feel the particles, as you are meant to, so you will notice you are carrying foreign debris and clear them out.

Your objective while you are on the earth is to clear the disharmonies, integrate the parts, and realign and reconnect to the source so Christ-like energy is pouring through you and out of you to remind others of their divine blueprint.

Cleansing your whole system with a clearing tool like RET is a process that clears the disharmonies out of you so that your divine power, spirit, and soul essence is established in every level of your being and you are guided completely by your spiritual higher self. Your body is a spirit body, your emotion is spirit emotion, and your mental powers are spirit mind. Your divine blueprint at every vibrational level is operating and active and continues to become increased and enlarged in wisdom and in stature.

Christ spent forty days in the wilderness to go through this process of becoming completely aligned and in harmony with God's will. When you achieve this restoration of wholeness in the physical body you have become like Christ, and when you meet him, you will know him. He is the template of our potential as humans to realize our god-self in the physical body. He has told us, "All these things you have seen me do ye will do also, even greater things than ye have seen me do, ye will do."[24] Our will becomes completely and effortlessly aligned with God's will because we are like him. Our system of energy reflects Christ's system of energy.

I believe that God and Christ have tangible physical bodies of flesh and bones. They are glorified beings with exalted bodies with all the powers and capacities of spirit at their disposal. We are meant to become like them: kings and queens, priests and priestesses of the most high, to rule and reign over a piece of the Universe with them. They are our mentors and tutors, our Father and our Brother. We knew them well. Many of us were taught by Christ when, as spirits, we walked with him in the light before our birth. Within the intelligence of your every cell, you remember this.

Claim your spiritual rights and privileges and choose to live a life of integrity, staying true to your sacred agreements and covenants so you can receive honor from on high. This earthly

[24] John 14:12.

state is a preparatory state. You came here to prepare yourself for something much grander and eternal. Be willing to move successfully through whatever you agreed would be required of you to receive your reward. It will be worth it and it doesn't have to be really hard anymore. Healing can occur quickly and easily if you will offer the faith to let that be your experience. The energy of Christ is so powerful with us, it is as if he were here. Choose to touch that energy as the woman touched his garment in the crowd and let that energy come into you and pass through you, and you will be healed.

The question is no longer, "Can a miracle occur?" We walk in the energy of miracles. The question is, "Do you have the courage to ask for a miracle and then the faith to let it occur, easily, gracefully, free of drama and struggle?" Let the energy of Christ, the power of the Atonement, grace your life daily. Ask in prayer:

Dear God, thank you for increasing my faith in the power of the Atonement. Through the energy of the Atonement, bless my life toward happiness and wellness this day. Thank you for helping me grow and remember who I am through joyous experiences. Thank you for assisting me in sustaining a vibration of wellness and joy in the name of Jesus Christ, amen.

Let wellness, peace of mind, hope, zest for life, and joyous emotion become your natural and familiar state.

CHAPTER *31*

FORGIVENESS IS NOT OPTIONAL

I used to believe that in some cases of traumatic life experience, forgiving might not be necessary in this lifetime. I no longer believe that. I believe every individual's life experience was divinely orchestrated to be perfect for that individual and forgiveness of anyone who hurts us in our journey is required if we want to graduate into higher states of light and truth. Our inability to forgive will keep us stuck, make us sick, and cause us to die eventually. The opposite of forgiveness is blame and resentment: two of the lowest vibratory states in which we can be. Forgiveness is a process of releasing us to the higher vibrations of gratitude and charity, the peace and love of Christ.

Forgiveness is the bridge that allows us to move into our Christ-consciousness. If you think you can get there without crossing that bridge, you are fooling yourself.

Christ was our human example of how to evoke godly characteristics within each of us. As he hung on the cross, having been wrongfully accused, and sentenced to a gruesome death by crucifixion, a few of his last words were, "Father, forgive them for they know not what they do."[25]

Christ, in his godlike awareness, knew that those who had ignored his innocence and condemned him to death were

---

[25] Luke 23:34.

playing a crucial part in the drama of the planet Earth. He knew their roles and felt gratitude that they would descend to such a level and deny their real selves. It is this example of forgiving that is required of us: releasing everyone in our life experience from any of our judgment and condemnation.

If you find it hard to forgive certain individuals in your life, you probably still believe that forgiveness condones what they have done to you. Let it go. Stop seeing what they have done to you as terrible. Start perceiving it as what you asked them to do so that you could use it as a means to overcome it, and to advance yourself spiritually. Seen in that light, there is nothing to forgive, only thanks to offer for how well they played their part.

*T*HERE IS ENOUGH MONEY FOR EVERYONE

Money is a system of energy. It is a neutral energy with a belief and perception we have each placed on it. Air is also energy, yet most people do not believe in a lack of air. When you breathe in air, do you panic because you fear that there may not be enough, so you better count your breaths to make sure you don't run out? Do you scold your children for taking in too many breaths and using too much air? Do you worry that you might run out of air at the end of the day, or week, or month? Probably not, but if you did, you would suffer from breathing difficulties and have to closely manage your air intake.

Most of the money we exchange everyday is no longer currency but numbers on a piece of paper. The amount of money you have or don't have is directly related to your beliefs about money. A lot of people believe there is not enough money, and their life reflects that belief. Every time you spend money, what feelings do you have? Do you feel good or feel worried? What thoughts run through your head? Do you worry you shouldn't be spending the money because you are thinking how much you do not have, or are you thinking: *I love to spend money because there is enough money for everyone and I always flow a lot into my life?*

Christ taught that it is easier for a poor man to enter into the Kingdom of Heaven than a rich man. I agree with this teaching because most people believe that when you are feeling poor, you are needy and are more likely to call upon powers higher than yourself to guide, instruct, and influence your life.

Christ did not say it was impossible for a rich man to enter into the Kingdom of Heaven, just that it would be harder. It is harder because most people carry deeper beliefs that continue to feed their perceptions that if we are too prosperous we will not be humble and obedient to God. Common beliefs around this include: *Love of money is the root of all evil. Rich people are not as spiritual. Only people who cheat have money. Money only comes from hard work.*

Because of our agency, we are free to create any belief we want. What if you were to believe: *I am wealthy and I am spiritual. I am allowing money to flow easily into my life and I am using it to enrich my life and the lives of others. I am wealthy and I am obedient to God's will for me. I am a humble, prosperous servant of the Lord. I am grateful for all the abundance that flows to me on all levels. I am healthy and experiencing a life of grace and ease and I am spiritual?* Every time we have an interaction with money, the Universe is giving us a chance to clear the deeper beliefs of not enough and the feeling of fear from our cells. Some people believe money comes easily and they will always have enough. Many people believe in a lack of money and continue to create an abundance of lack. The people who have come to me with money issues and poverty consciousness have beliefs about money that keep them lacking. These beliefs include:

- ❖ I will never make enough money.
- ❖ I am always in debt.
- ❖ My parents never had enough and I never will, either.
- ❖ Artists and creative people have to struggle. Money only comes from hard work.
- ❖ Money always goes out faster than it comes in.
- ❖ I am always worrying about money because there is never enough.

Many of the clients I have worked with also have beliefs about money that are woven into their spiritual beliefs. Some common beliefs about money and their spiritual status include:

- ❖ Money is filthy and dirty.
- ❖ Money is evil.
- ❖ I am poor, but righteous.
- ❖ Rich people are crooks.
- ❖ There are too many poor people for me to deserve wealth.
- ❖ Only people who cheat have money.
- ❖ I have a fear of being greedy.
- ❖ Rich people are wicked.
- ❖ Poverty keeps me humble.

If you are experiencing a lack of money and the experience of managing money is a constant struggle that you regularly wrestle with in your mind, you have deeper beliefs and patterns with money that are keeping you stuck in a state of lacking.

Poverty consciousness can be easily changed to prosperity consciousness by clearing your deeper beliefs and replacing them with new beliefs. Some of the new beliefs that will assist you in creating more wealth and prosperity include:

  ❖ I recognize prosperity everywhere and rejoice in it fully. There is plenty for me.

  ❖ The abundance of the Universe is available to everyone—including me.

  ❖ I attract money easily; there is always more money coming in than going out.

  ❖ I spend money wisely and comfortably.

  ❖ I am open and receptive to new avenues of income.

  ❖ Money is my friend. I enjoy my experience with it.

  ❖ I am comfortable with large sums of money.

  ❖ I am using money to bless my life and others.

  ❖ I am wealthy and I am generous and spiritual.

  ❖ I am a money magnet, and I am attracting my piece of the prosperity that God has provided for everyone.

  ❖ I am worthy and deserving of large sums of money.

  ❖ I continuously rejoice in and bless the good fortune of everyone.

As well as establishing new beliefs, you will create some new behaviors with money. If someone were to ask you, "Do you have any money?" What would be your most common response? If it is frequently "No," then you are telling the Universe you have no money and you will continue to have no money. Always carry money in your wallet or billfold. Always be able to answer, "Yes, I have money. I have plenty of money."

That is the message that will help you create more money. Whenever you spend money, notice how you feel. If you feel uncomfortable and nervous because you are worried that the money you are spending might not be replaced, the signal you are sending out is one of lack, and lack will be returned to you.

When you spend money, create a positive, peaceful feeling. Trust that as you spend money, you create a vacuum for more money to come into your life. Always stay within your current means of income and at the same time create a vibration of prosperity to create more coming in the future. Every time you pay your bills, be in the energy of gratitude that you have creditors that trust you and offer you their services. Acquire sound money-management skills to assist you in staying in integrity with your money.

When you communicate about money, do you talk about not having enough and focus your words on lack and struggle with money? Notice your communication patterns with money and choose to speak positively and reference your state of abundance with money. Do you trust your family members and perceive them as capable and competent when it comes to spending money? Or do you fear that they will create debt and spend more than you have so you need to control them? Create perceptions and language that reflect a state of prosperity consciousness rather than poverty consciousness.

The Universe does not know your bank account status; it only reads the signals you are feeding it. So create a vibration of wealth by playing the following game:

Pretend you have an unlimited supply of $100 bills in your wallet. Every time you spend a $100 bill, imagine another one *magically replacing it. Throughout your day, think of the many things you could spend that $100 on. Act as if you are spending it over and over and over. Rejoice and have fun with all the things you could buy, all the people you could share it with, and all the experiences you could create. As you do this you will send out a vibration of wealth and prosperity that will assist you in creating more wealth.*

As you shift into a vibration of prosperity consciousness, you will create and attract new avenues and opportunities for more money to come into your life. Money is a resource that God has given us to bless our lives, not to interfere with our daily happiness. If you are creating your experience with money as a negative distraction, choose to clean it up. Create money to be like your experience with air: something you know there is plenty of for you and everyone else. Money, like air, is a resource to assist you in creating and sustaining a life of joy and happiness. You never worry about air, you just trust and let it be there for you. Stop worrying about money and start trusting that you will be provided for and trust that you will make choices and manage it in a way that blesses your life.

CHAPTER 53

The Universe Is Abundant

The Universe is the place in which we live. The Universe is the realm of God and all that he has created and all that he has yet to create. I used to think of the planet Earth as my home with all of its occupants as my community. I now think of the Universe as my home and all of its occupants as my community. Much of the Universe exists as unorganized matter waiting to be organized into a creation. Deepak Chopra calls this subatomic material the unified field or the "field of all possibilities." [26] We are all connected to this unified field and it is the origin of all our creations.

Abundance is the natural state of the Universe. The Universe can only respond to us in abundance. We always receive what we believe in abundantly. Abundance is merely the Universe's response to our thoughts and feelings. The Universe provides experience in abundance to assist us in becoming aware of what we are thinking and feeling.

The Universe is energy with potential, waiting for instructions from us. We are connected to this fluid energy and we are always creating something with it. **We can only create in abundance.**

---

[26] Deepak Chopra. *The A-to-Z Steps to a Richer Life*. New York, NY: Barnes and Noble. 1993. pg.3.

$\mathscr{S}$ERVING OTHERS HELPS US REMEMBER OUR WHOLENESS

What you give to another, you give to yourself: what goes around comes around. Service to others, free of anything given in return, is high-quality giving. Giving of our time and talents to better someone else's life returns the good we have given at least tenfold to us. There is no need to worry about what you are going to get back. You only need to worry about what you are going to give out. Life is about the highest-quality giving, not the highest-quality getting.

When you give someone love and support, you give yourself love and support. As you validate someone's self-worth, you validate your self-worth. As you forgive another, you forgive yourself and are forgiven. As you recognize the higher self and wholeness within another, you recognize and remember this truth within yourself.

Give of yourself willingly and in the tone of appreciation. If you give with an attitude of complaining and resentment, you cut yourself off from the flow of goodness that wants to return to you. Give because you choose to, not because you need to, have to, or should. Christ said, "Love one another; as I have loved you, that ye also love one another." [27] How has he loved

27 John 13:34.

us? He has loved us willingly, generously, free of any judgments, always allowing what we choose to create. Love others willingly, generously, and free of any judgment. See others as you see yourself: doing the best they know how to do in that moment.

The Universe orchestrates opportunities for us to serve others. If we turn the opportunities away, we turn ourselves away. Use your power of discernment to choose opportunities that have been perfectly orchestrated on your behalf to assist you in remembering your wholeness.

Whatever qualities and capacities of spirit you want to increase, ask the Holy Spirit to orchestrate opportunities for you to exercise those qualities in serving others. As you act as if you already possess those qualities, the Universe will return to you the essence of those qualities multiplied. Those qualities will integrate within you and become you.

Change yourself by serving others. Be your highest self. Act the part and you will become the part. There is enough: *enough time, enough love,* and *enough money.* As this knowledge increases and organizes within you, giving of yourself becomes a sacred act that recognizes the *Christ* in all of us.

THE POWER OF APPRECIATION AND GRATITUDE

Appreciate everything. Express gratitude for every single moment of your life. The more you create feelings of appreciation and gratitude, the more you will attract into your life that which you can appreciate and for which you can feel gratitude.

Gratitude is one of the highest vibrations in which we can be. Look for things for which you can be grateful. As you're driving along, play the "Grateful Game." By yourself or with others, take turns saying what you are grateful for. Start a Gratitude Journal. Every Thanksgiving, as a family, we get out our Gratitude Journal and write 1,000 things for which we are grateful. We number from one to 1,000, leave it on the kitchen counter with a pen, and family members and friends are invited to write in it as often as they would like. It usually takes us between a week and ten days to get to 1,000.

In your prayers, thank God for believing in you, for giving you the agency to create your life, and for remembering your truth. Thank all the people who have shown up in your life to play parts.

Write a thank-you note once a week to someone to express your appreciation for them. Appreciate yourself for what you are remembering and for the joys you are creating.

In Christ-consciousness, we can only look at our life and the world through the eyes of gratitude. All blame, anger, resentment, frustration, and all other negative beliefs and emotions melt away. Feed the energy of gratitude within you. If you are stuck, say the following prayer:

Dear God, thank you for awakening and connecting within me my state of gratitude. Thank you for influencing my perceptions so that I only see my life and the people in it through the eyes of appreciation and gratitude. Thank you for loving and appreciating me. In the name of Jesus Christ, amen.

CHAPTER

The Test Is Ending

We came into life believing that struggle and pain are the medium for growth and spiritual advancement. We live in a time when we can grow and learn through joy and love, and we no longer have to struggle. It has been purposeful to know pain. It has been purposeful to know heartache, rejection, hatred, judgment, and difficulties that challenged our very souls. We have created a world where enough people have been abused, enough people have been killed, enough people have been judged, ridiculed, and mocked. We have brought pain and struggle to a glorious finale here in the last days of our test on earth.

What has the test been? The test has been to confront ourselves with the greatest amount of human carnage we possibly could throughout the history of civilization, and see if we would come out of it with our goodness predominantly intact. We came to earth to learn if we could prevail over that which had the power to destroy us. We knew that the earth had the contrast of good and evil, and we were given the power to choose which forces to create our lives with. We knew in order to know the one, we must know the other.

We no longer need to create the pain. The test is ending. We have succeeded and life as we have known it is changing. We are experiencing some big final episodes of violent and painful events that are getting the attention of the entire world. The youth and children are playing out a big script to help us get it. When our children start killing and hurting each other, we really sit up, pay attention, and take accountability for our choices and start looking at what we don't want and what kind of world we do want.

This is assisting us in completing these old painful patterns by helping us become aware that *enough is enough* and we don't want it anymore. It is helping us have discussions with each other about what kind of world we do want to live in. It is helping us talk more openly and honestly to our spouses and our children about the environment we want to create. It is bringing people together with the intention to create a peaceful world.

We can, individually and as families, graduate from struggle and pain to a life of peace, prosperity, grace, and ease. We do not need to wait until our governments choose this. God is helping us to prepare the earth for the return of his son and our elder brother and Savior, Jesus Christ. When Christ returns to the earth, he will graduate us to even greater levels of light and truth. We are meant to live in prosperity, love, peace, charity, compassion, joy, and affluence. As more and more of us prepare ourselves, we will be more able to live in harmony with the energy and lifestyle patterns of a Christ-culture.

Struggle and pain have been our means to know the mastery of our souls and the capacity to ultimately choose good over evil. We came believing we could triumph over the negative, evil forces—and we have. There are more people choosing to live

Christ-like lives than people choosing to create evil lives. At times it may not seem like it because the media bombards us with stories of violence, carnage, and every inhumane act possible. The media takes the experiences of the minority and sends the message that it is happening to the majority. This is not true. There is a dominance of love and brotherly kindness on the planet. Don't buy into the doom and gloom. Keep your sights set on the light that radiates from so many of God's children.

God wants us to know that he loves us and is very pleased with what we have created here on earth. We have a way to go, but the good news is we are moving in an accelerated fashion into higher states of consciousness and more and more levels of light and intelligence. This we have chosen for ourselves. The other option, which we did not choose, was to move into greater levels of darkness until we mass-destructed. This will not happen. If we were to say there has been a war here on earth between the forces of good and evil, we could say at this time that good is winning and will ultimately prevail.

To create more power and accelerate the good, keep your attention on the good that is happening in your world. Create kind acts towards others every day. Look for all the good that surrounds you. Acknowledge in gratitude your remarkable and wonderful life, the miracle of your existence, and praise the glory of the time in which you live. There has never been a more exciting time to live on the earth. To be here for the final episodes of the plan of good and evil and to have the opportunity to usher in a new millennium, one in which Christ will come home to the planet he helped create, is very, very exciting indeed.

REMEMBERING OUR FUTURE

As a result of the attacks that occurred on the United States on September 11, 2001, I hear more frequently, "We are scared. We are not sure what is going to happen."

• My response to that is, "What do you want to happen?" We do have a choice. We are not victims living in a world of random events. We have various futures available to us individually and collectively. Fear will take us into a future with more pain and tragedy. Love and hope will take us into a future with a world where peace and prosperity abound.

Since September 11, 2001, we are each in a position bigger than we have ever been in to choose which future we will experience.

Stephen Hawkings, one of the most brilliant minds of our time, made a curious comment about our future. He was explaining the nature of the past, present, and future all happening simultaneously in the cosmic scheme of things. If this is the case, our past, our present, and our future are already in existence for us. He commented that since our future already exists and we can remember the past, why are we not also remembering the future?

Since hearing that, I have set an intention to remember and live the future that offers me the greatest success in accomplishing my purpose here on the earth.

Have you contemplated what it might look like to remember your future? What are the thoughts and feelings like? What does it sound like to ask God to help you remember your future?

As we set an intention to be aligned with our best possible future, we put ourselves on track to manifest it.

Ask to remember your future and share with me how this is developing for you.

CHAPTER

I BELIEVE IN CHRIST

Christ suffered, so we would not have to. In the Garden of Gethsemane, Christ took upon himself all the sins of mankind and released any power this energy had to keep us stuck in our suffering state. In this single event, Christ took upon himself all of the negative, heavy energy that had been and ever would be created by mankind, and recycled it back into light energy. This powerful act of atonement allowed us to reclaim our oneness with Christ and the Christ within us.

If Christ, being a God like our Father in Heaven, had not come to earth to receive a physical body to perform this one of many great acts of service, we would be powerless and unable to awaken to higher states of consciousness. We would never have advanced spiritually as a human race and probably would have destroyed ourselves by this time. Christ's atonement is one of the single most important acts ever performed by a mortal, here on this earth. He suffered greatly, so much that as this dark, heavy energy poured through his physical frame, he bled at every pore.

Christ's atonement has already healed us. It is our belief in struggle and our patterns of recreating upset and drama in our lives that keep us from maintaining this healed state. We believe that we have to be punished for our misdeeds and often block the powers of Christ's atonement in our behalf. We create our own agenda of punishment, believing we are unworthy.

⌇

Larry was a divorced father of four children. He blamed himself and his inadequacies as a husband and father for the break-up of his marriage and family. He believed he could never do enough to please those he loved, so naturally he attracted a woman into his life that was never pleased with his efforts. These patterns eventually lead to her leaving him and the four children. It was a year after his divorce when he came to see me. He wanted to meet other women and yet would not allow himself this pleasure, because at a deeper level he believed he was unworthy and needed to be punished for breaking up his family. He was not allowing the powers of the Atonement to come into him and heal him because he believed he needed to be punished longer.

After releasing the need to punish himself, he turned to the spiritual powers that are available to all of us, and asked to receive them. His life took a wonderful new direction, and he was accelerated in his healing work. Within the next year, he met a woman who believed in him because he now believed in himself. They were married the next year and are successfully blending two families together.

Another client, Bob, was just a dissertation paper away from receiving his doctorate. He kept putting it off and creating many excuses instead of completing it. In his sessions, he discovered that he was not allowing himself to finish it because it was a means of punishing himself for disappointing his father years ago, for dropping out of college and, in his father's words, "wasting his money." Bob felt unworthy of this honor and deprived himself of this achievement out of self-inflicted punishment. He did not believe he could call upon the powers of the Atonement to assist him with completing it until his self-imposed sentencing was complete.

If the Atonement has already healed us, why do we feel so bad at times or make life so hard? Because in that moment of feeling bad, or in the struggle, we are denying ourselves of this power and putting our attention on the problem. If we would put our attention on the solution, without even having to know what it is, we would manifest it.

As we each receive the power of the Atonement into our lives, we allow a literal force of God to move through us and awaken the solutions within us to organize and be formed into conscious linear thought. These thoughts are fresh, new ideas that are the solutions we have been seeking. Our thoughts are matched with compelling feelings to move us into inspired action and we find ourselves effortlessly thinking and doing that which creates more harmony and happiness in our lives. We are blessed with the capacity to move out of our difficult situation into a place of light and truth.

We need to understand that the power of the Atonement is available to us in our lives now; it enables us to heal our lives of all pain and suffering. The Atonement has the power to restore every loss, dry every tear, and heal every pain we create. The answers to complete healing and permanent recovery are found in the atonement of Jesus Christ. I believe the powers and gifts of the Atonement can heal you so completely that you will have the freedom to live the rest of your life as if you had never suffered or struggled.

The power of the atonement of Jesus Christ is real. The power of faith in his atonement is real. As we live by faith in the atonement of Jesus Christ, this faith provides us with the power and energy to heal ourselves. Christ's atonement can bless our lives despite the bitterness or the adversity of our past trials. Ask to have this force released into your life with the following prayer:

Thank you, God, for flowing the powers of the Atonement into my life to awaken the Christ that is within me. I ask that these powers activate the patterns of well-being and wholeness that lie dormant in me. Thank you for integrating these patterns into all levels of my being so that I am free to create a life of joy and prosperity in all things. Thank you for assisting me in knowing that I am already healed. Help me to receive this healing with grace and ease. In the name of Jesus Christ, amen.

The power of the Atonement works in our lives as an incremental process, line upon line, grace to grace. The Atonement is a gift that we must receive, but receiving it is not a passive act. To receive more fully the gift of the Atonement we must ask for it and believe it can change our lives, effortlessly.

The Atonement of Jesus Christ is the essence and core of his gospel. The word gospel means "good news," and one of the most important parts of the "good news" of the Atonement comes to us in the form of grace. I believe the power of Christ's divine grace, made available by his act of Atonement, can do more for our lives than any other spiritual power available to us.

One of the meanings of grace is receiving unmerited divine assistance. Christ's act of atonement released a powerful force into the energy fields of this planet and it is available to each of us in the form of grace. We each have available to us divine help and strength given through the bounteous mercy and love of Jesus Christ. It is through the grace of the Lord that we receive strength and assistance to do what we would otherwise not be able to do, if left to our own means. This grace is an enabling power that allows us to lay hold onto eternal life and exaltation after we have expended our own best efforts.

Because Christ took on all dark and disharmonious energies, I am free to clear any dark energy that I carry. As I clear these dark energies, I am filled with the light of Christ to restore me to wholeness. As I am filled with more light, I am able to sustain greater levels of faith, which allow me to create more of what I want and manifest more spontaneous miracles in my life.

As we keep the commandments and our sacred agreements with God, the Atonement releases the forces of grace into our lives. Just as Christ progressed and received grace for grace until he received fullness, we too receive grace for grace. We heal and mature into higher states of consciousness as we keep his commandments, until we will receive a fullness of his light. In this we are restored to our natural state of wholeness.

Through the grace of Christ, through his divine assistance, we become empowered, endowed with strength, hope, courage, and other spiritual gifts we specifically need to be successful in all aspects of life. Through the grace of Christ, we will be allowed to reenter God's presence endowed with the attributes that we have worked so hard to acquire in diligent efforts to become like him.

I believe the power of grace is available and given to everyone. As you strive to live in harmony with Christ's teachings, you can experience Christ's flowing powers of grace which will come into your being and work within you, assisting you daily in your life.

Come unto Christ and align your will with God's will. Come unto Christ and become God-reliant as well as self-reliant. Come unto Christ and build your spiritual foundation on the rock of Christ's Atonement.

Turn to the Savior in your life. I believe there is no greater source of help than in coming unto Christ. He will show you the way. Through his influence you will be able to make choices that will serve your highest good. He will give you strength and hope to change your life, so that you may bring yourself to a new life—one filled with love, peace, success, and joy.

Christ is returning to the earth that he helped create. We live in a time where we are more free to come unto him, so we can be like him. We are learning to live like him, so we can live with him.

In sessions, I invite clients to close their eyes and imagine themselves in the light with Christ. *Once you have closed your eyes, tell your mind to go to the place where Christ is. See yourself standing in the light with Christ. You are both adorned in robes of white and brilliant light. It feels good to stand in the light with your brother and friend. He reaches out to you and invites you to be held by him. Imagine Christ has something to give you. He is waiting to give you his gift, but first you must give him the burdens you are carrying. Imagine a heavy pack on your back or a large boulder you are carrying. Christ invites you to drop the burdens you have been carrying at his feet. He invites you to turn around and see all the generations that came before you and how many of them carried the same burdens. Christ tells them all to approach and drop their burdens. As everyone lets go of their burden, they are now free to receive a gift from Christ. Go to him and receive your gift. Notice the gift for you and place it in your heart.*

Thank Christ for loving you unconditionally and for always being there to support and guide you. Imagine all this energy coming into your body and being released into every part of you. Notice your whole body from the top of your head to the tip of your toes, and tell your body that this feeling of peace is familiar and natural. Sit quietly basking in the light of Christ.

CHAPTER 59

*T*HERE IS A CHRIST IN ALL OF US

Everyone has the blueprint within them to *become Christ*—literally become like Christ. Christ is our human template for the potential of our human biology. I believe Christ had all the dynamics of his biology fully active and operating. His entire DNA was fully functioning. One hundred percent of his brain was active. The blueprints for wholeness on all levels of his being were turned on and operating.

We are not only meant to become like Christ in thoughts and deed, we have the potential to become like Christ biologically. He had mastered his thought processes so that he never thought a negative thought. Thought and completion were real for Christ. Whatever he thought manifested itself immediately. He had the power to command the elements with his mind. He had the power to influence the subatomic particles of this dimension to be rearranged to create different states. To heal people, he commanded the elements to return to a pattern that reflected wholeness and recovery to the individuals he assisted.

Brigham Young said, "The Savior converted the water into wine. He knew how to call the necessary elements together in order to fill the water with the properties of wine. The elements are all around us; we eat, drink, and breathe them, and Jesus, understanding the process of calling them together, performed no miracle except to those who were ignorant of that process. It was the same with the woman who was healed by touching the hem of his garment [see Matthew 9:20-22]; she was healed by faith, but it was no miracle to Jesus. He understood the process, and although he was pressed by the crowd, behind and before, and on each side, so that he could scarcely make his way through it, the moment she touched him, he felt virtue leave him and inquired who touched him. This was no miracle to him. He had the issues of life and death in his power; he had power to lay down his life and power to take it up again [see John 10:17-18]." [28]

Jesus had the power in and of himself; the Father had given it to him; it was his legacy. He had the streams and issues of life within him. When he said, "live," people lived. This is our same legacy. God has given us the same potential power. Christ told us that the things we had seen him do, we would also do.[29] Author and speaker Greg Braden teaches us that as we continue to awaken to higher states of consciousness and to evolve biologically, we will discover that the technology outside of us is just to remind us of what exists within us as the potential of our humanness.

Consider the possibility that as enough of us continue to remember our wholeness, the collective consciousness of all of us will ascend into a higher state of Christ-awareness. In this state of awareness, our physical bodies begin to ascend into higher and higher levels of vibration. As we move through this sanctification process, more of our DNA and

[28] Brigham Young. *Teachings of the Presidents of the Church.* pg. 256.
[29] John 14:12.

our brain function are activated. With more of our biology turned on, we will have a body like Christ's, with all the powers and capacities that he had. He is our model as a human on how to master our thoughts and how to use this power to live in harmony to create more and more of that which adds joy to our experience on this earth.

As the Christ-powers within you are awakened, set an intention that you will use these powers with wisdom and integrity, seeking to align your will with God's, just as Christ did.

CHARITY: THE PURE LOVE OF CHRIST

A state of charity is one of the highest vibrations we can achieve. Charity is unconditional love: the pure love of Christ. To obtain charity, we are sanctified and purified of all human tendencies to do all things that counter joy: hate, fear, and judgment of others and ourselves. This makes us one energy with Christ.

We each choose life experiences that evoke within us the parts of us that carry impurities. These impurities are a veil that keeps us from remembering and knowing our only real truth: that we are whole and healed, and we always were.

In a state of charity, our minds become single to God, and our will is the Father's will. In this state we can never ask amiss, and all that we ask for will be given. Our spirit self has subdued our physical self, and our soul and body are one. The spirit of God unites with our spirit and becomes our congenial companion; the mind and will of God are transmitted to us. Albert Einstein once said, "I want to know the thoughts of God; everything else is details."

In a state of charity, we know the thoughts of God. We are connected to the light of Christ so completely, it is as if the light of heaven and the thoughts of God communicate to our intelligence directly.

In this state of charity, there is only a desire to do good. Our joy is full because we only choose to create that which brings more joy. Our lessons and awareness come through joyful rather than painful experiences. We are humble and submissive because we choose to be. We hold a reverence for ourselves, for our divine worth, and for everyone and everything else on the planet.

I believe we each hold a blueprint within us for being in a state of charity: a state of pure and unconditional love. If we choose to submit ourselves to the guidelines and instructions the Lord requires of us and himself, then obtaining this state of charity is our rightful inheritance. To be accountable for our creations and to live in integrity with God's laws is the means to receive the grace of God and, after all we can do, to graduate to this glorified state.

Love your life. Love the process of remembering your wholeness. Have fun along the way. We are eternal beings, so we never stop progressing. There is no destination, just more opportunities to create from higher levels of light. If you're not experiencing joy in the journey, you're missing out on one of the main reasons for being here.

Remember you are loved. You can be, do, and have anything you can imagine and hold the vibration to create. Go for it. God wants you to be successful. You have his help and a whole legion of angels ready and waiting to assist you. Use this help. Keep the heavens really busy as you create more joy. Help others remember their wholeness, and together desire more love and create more joy.

AFTERWORD
ALL THIS WILL TAKE PRACTICE

This book has been written as a handbook, a guide, and reference book. It is a book that I am still learning from. I have written what I believe are the possibilities for us now and increasingly in the future. Refer to it often, use the prayers and self-help processes frequently. Take one section a week for a year and read, study, and implement the principles and tools that are taught. Read the Table of Contents daily to awaken these truths within you. Allow the healing powers of Christ to flow through this book to you.

In every moment, during every day of your life, you have choices. The choice to create more struggle or the choice to create more freedom and joy. Choose thoughts that support you in feeling good more and more each day.

It will take practice to gain mastery over your thoughts and feelings. Never give up. Never settle for mediocrity. You can accomplish more than you think. Just because we have not achieved this state of learning in joy, rather than pain, does not mean it is not possible. **I believe it is possible. I believe it is our destiny.**

APPENDIX OF PRAYERS

A Prayer to Change Your Perception (see page 97)

Thank you, God, for blessing me with a perception of my current experience that supports me in feeling good. I ask that through the power of Christ's atonement all my cells will be cleared of the negative beliefs and feelings that are keeping me stuck in this perception. This I ask in the name of Jesus Christ, amen.

A Prayer to Ask for Ministering Angels (see page 139)

Thank you, God, for sending healing angels to minister over me tonight. To assist me in clearing, healing, and awakening on all levels while I am sleeping. I am experiencing my real self more clearly, presently, and focused in my day-to-day life. I ask for this in the name of Jesus Christ, amen.

A Prayer to Become Aware of Spiritual Contracts (see page 195)

Dear God, thank you for revealing to my conscious mind what my spiritual agreements and contracts are. I desire to be engaged in them and to create successful outcomes so that I am an instrument in thy hands to bless my life and others', in the name of Jesus Christ, amen.

A Prayer of Complete Gratitude (see page 214)

Thank you, God, for watching over me and my loved ones and for keeping us safe this day. Thank you for the good experiences I am going to have today. Thank you for all the money that is coming my way and for my wisdom in using it, and that I am having fun with my experience with it. Thank you for assisting my business in becoming more successful. Thank you for the opportunities that are being orchestrated on my behalf to further my work here on the earth.

Thank you for forgiving me and always loving me. Thank you for always being there for me. Thank you for flowing the energy of the Atonement to me to bless my life this day, and for the power of thy Grace to assist me in being more of who I really am. I love thee and appreciate thee, and say this in the name of Jesus Christ, amen.

A Prayer to Empower your Children (see page 257)

Dear God, thank you for watching over my children and keeping them safe. Thank you for helping me see their higher selves. I pray that as they make choices that are disharmonious to their core desires, the results of these choices will return to them magnified and they will know and feel discomfort if it is not what they want. As they make choices that are harmonious with their core desires, the results will be magnified, and they will notice and feel tremendous peace. Thank you for helping me be sensitive to their needs. Fill me with inspiration to know what to say and when to say it, so they will know their great worth. Thank you for reminding me to hug them and to look them in the eyes when we are interacting. Thank you for orchestrating more opportunities that will create more feelings of love, trust, honor, and playfulness between us. I love playing with my children. Thank you for all the grand adventures we have had, and for the many more that are coming. Thank you, God, for watching over and sending ministering angels to their future spouses to help prepare them for my children so they can come together and create joyful families. In the name of Jesus Christ, amen.

A Prayer to Increase Faith in the Power of the Atonement (see page 271)

Dear God, thank you for increasing my faith in the power of the Atonement. Through the energy of the Atonement, bless my life towards happiness and wellness this day. Thank you for helping me grow and remember who I am through joyous experiences. Thank you for assisting me in sustaining a vibration of wellness and joy, in the name of Jesus Christ, amen.

A Prayer to Experience the World in Gratitude (see page 286)

Dear God, thank you for awakening and connecting within me my state of gratitude. Thank you for influencing my perceptions so that I only see my life and the people in it through the eyes of appreciation and gratitude. Thank you for loving and appreciating me. In the name of Jesus Christ, amen.

A Prayer to Call Upon the Powers of the Atonement to Heal Your Life (see page 296)

Thank you, God, for flowing the powers of the Atonement into my life to awaken the Christ that is within me. I ask that these powers activate the patterns of well-being and wholeness that lie dormant in me. Thank you for integrating these patterns into all levels of my being so that I am free to create a life of joy and prosperity in all things. Thank you for assisting me in knowing that I am already healed. Help me to receive this healing with grace and ease. In the name of Jesus Christ, amen.

APPENDIX OF SELF-HELP PROCESSES

Being in the Light with Christ

In sessions, I invite clients to close their eyes and imagine themselves in the light with Christ. *Once you have closed your eyes, tell your mind to go to the place where Christ is. See yourself standing in the light with Christ. You are both adorned in robes of white and brilliant light. It feels good to stand in the light with your brother and friend. He reaches out to you and invites you to be held by him. Imagine Christ has something to give you. He is waiting to give you his gift, but first you must first give him the burdens you are carrying. Imagine a heavy pack on your back or a large boulder you are carrying. Christ invites you to drop the burdens you have been carrying at his feet. He invites you to turn around and see all the generations that came before you and how many of them carried the same burdens. Christ tells them all to approach and drop their burdens. As everyone lets go of their burden, they are now free to receive a gift from Christ. Go to him and receive your gift. Notice the gift for you and place it in your heart.*

Thank Christ for loving you unconditionally and for always being there to support and guide you. Imagine all this energy coming into your body and being released into every part of you. Notice your whole body from the top of your head to the tip of your toes, and tell your body that this feeling of peace is familiar and natural. Sit quietly basking in the light of Christ.

Petitioning Your Angels

Start by deciding what you want in your life. An easy writing process to help you become clearer in knowing what you want is to identify first what you don't want. Take a piece of paper and on one side list "What I Don't Want." On the other side list "What I Do Want." Ask yourself the question, *If my life were ideal, what would it look like?*

I tell my clients that if God were to come to you and say, "George, you can have your life be any way you want it to be. Tell me how you want it to be, and I'll help you create it." What would you tell God? I counsel the person to only imagine what they can honestly believe is possible for them. If they do not believe it could happen easily, they will doubt. Doubt energy is a heavy energy that disconnects us from source energy. This creates resistance on our part, which interferes with allowing what we have asked for to manifest easily.

In this process write the ideal you really believe could happen. List desires that include your relationships, career, body, mind, state of abundance, home, transportation, and spiritual and family life. Or take one of these areas and list what you want in detail. Remember, the more specifically you ask for what you want, the more specifically you will receive it.

Deciding what you want is the first step in setting into motion the creation of what you want. The second step that allows it to come effortlessly into your life is to play a game I call "Ask Your Angels."

Take your list, all or part, and write at the top, "Thank you for orchestrating the details for the following desires to come into my life effortlessly and joyfully." Close your eyes and imagine a spiritual crew receiving your requests and going to work to make them happen for you. Your job now is to want it, believe it, allow it, and appreciate it. It will happen.

Protecting Yourself from Negative Energy

1. When you start feeling negative, then you have your thoughts on what you don't want and/or you are making choices that are leading you to what you don't want. Pay attention to the negative emotion. Stop and ask your spirit-self and God: *What am I currently thinking, believing, or choosing that is causing me to feel bad?* Stay quiet and you will receive the answer. As you practice this more and more, you will receive your answers with more and more clarity. This knowledge will be accompanied by a distinct higher vibration that when continually honored will become more and more clear for you. If you ignore the negative emotion and keep doing what is causing you to feel bad, little by little you will subdue the powers of your spirit-self and the Holy Spirit from having an effect on you. You cut yourself off from your guidance system.

2. When you notice negative energy around people or in the place where you are, ask for angels to come and create a vortex of light to remove the negative energy and recycle it into light energy. Many people unconsciously take on heavy, negative energy to help others feel better or to clear out disharmonies in the places they've been during the day. They feel tired much of the time and have a hard time feeling positive. Many of the

negative emotions they are feeling are not even their own. Become aware of energies outside of yourself and ask for spiritual assistance to clear it so you are not part of the process of channeling the negative energy.

3. If you sense negative emotions that are not your own, ask to be surrounded by white and gold light. Ask the Holy Spirit to send angels to the place you are going or to the place you are to clear any negative energies and to surround everyone present with white and gold light. You do not need to take on the negative energies of others. Let spirit do it for you.

Releasing Old Energy Patterns

When you notice you are in an old energy pattern, say to yourself: *I must have wanted to experience this again. I am forgiving myself for thinking I deserve this. I am choosing to live in the new energy of me. I am loved, supported, and now learning and growing through joyous experiences. I am experiencing that what I want is good and I can have it easily and effortlessly.*

Daily Script to Have a Better Day

Read the following script daily and watch your life change:

It's amazing how well my day goes. It is as if the Universe knows who I am and what I want and things flow to me in such a timely way. It is as if I'm dancing with the Universe.

Emergencies are nonexistent in my physical experience. The people that come to me are benefiting by their exposure to me. It is as if I have a secretary in the sky that is taking care of everything and just feeding it to me with such ease and grace and comfort that my day just flows and unfolds so magnificently.

When I wake up in the morning, I am infused with the energy of well-being. I'm just glad to be alive. I can hardly wait to exercise my body and I am thankful for the time I can spend with my children.

When they awaken, my children and spouse are joyful and happy to be alive and we have such fun interacting with one another. This is some of the most precious time of our day as we embark upon our day together—positively anticipating what will unfold.

As I am making my way to different events of my day, it is always such a lovely time. I am so appreciative of all the wonderful people I have in my life. I am grateful for the spiritual support and the angelic help that is taking care of the details and making sure that this day is going to unfold in a magical way.

I love seeing their attention to detail, and I love seeing them eagerly finding more ways to make everything go comfortably. I love recognizing that they're helping me bring my life into balance.

I love being a wife/husband. I love being a mom/dad. I love getting into a space wherein I realize that I can deal with anything. I love connecting with the infinite power and knowledge of my life. I love knowing the benefit I offer to others. Most of all, I love the joy of the unfolding. I love new surprises that come, my ability to move with them, and the inspiration that comes to me effortlessly. I love knowing that I can participate in anything I want to participate in. I love knowing I have infinite choices.

Tell the Universe the way you want it to be! Even if you have to stretch it a little bit. The Universe doesn't know the difference.

Staying in Unconditional Love

Have you ever had the experience of talking to someone, or listening to music and being present in a particular environment and you felt all warm and fuzzy inside? As if someone were hugging you on the inside? You did not want this experience to end because you did not want the feeling to leave. This is what it feels like to be held in the energy of unconditional love. God wants to share it with everyone and he will if we just ask. He has told us, "Ask and ye shall receive." If I am asking for myself, I say, *Thank you, God, for encircling me in the arms of your love.* I imagine I am surrounded in a bubble of white light and angels are anointing me. I can lie in my bed in the morning and feel enclosed by a very warm and tender energy that is holding me. If I am asking for others I say, *Thank you, God, for flowing your love into the presence of this individual person or group of people.* Since this energy is unbounded, unrestricted, and unlimited, you can play with it in a big way to affect a lot of people at once.

The next time you are at a very large event, like a play, concert, or sporting event, ask for this energy to flow to everyone in attendance and for the Heavens to part and angels to come down and minister to all present. Do you get the picture? Do you realize the powers of Heaven you have at your disposal? Do you realize that when you ask, you receive, and what you have asked for is manifest, and in that asking you are changing the world?

Creating Opportunities to Share Love with Your Children

Ask angels to orchestrate opportunities every day for you to affirm your children. Moments will occur when you will be filled with loving energy and the words that will flow easily to affirm their great worth. Even if your children are adults, they will still love to hear these messages from you. Ask angels to orchestrate moments in your phone calls and interactions where it will happen naturally. If you have little or no contact with your children, choose to send these messages to their subconscious minds and the energy of your love to surround them.

You Can Change Instantly

The next time you are feeling stuck in a place of feeling bad, ask God to bless you with an understanding and a perception of your experience that will invite and awaken peaceful soothing feelings inside of you. Be willing to clear the negative beliefs and feelings by asking to have these cleared from the deepest parts of your cells.

Physical Healing

1. A healthy expression that supports us in dealing with the disharmonies we have become aware of is to say, "My

body has experienced the condition of _____

in the past, and now I choose to get the message it has

for me, clear the disharmonies, claim my real self and

move on." This statement accurately describes the sit-

uation without making it your current identity, puts it in

the past, takes responsibility for clearing the disharmonies

causing the imbalance, and exercises faith to heal.

2. If you are suffering with physical ailments, find the
    emotional and mental origin of them. You will experience
    increased results and more powers of healing at the phys-
    ical level as you let go of your repressed negative
    emotions and limiting beliefs.

3. If it is a part of your divine plan to heal, use your faith
    to receive the gift of healing and you will. If it is your
    time to move on to spirit, come to terms with this and
    go in peace. Either way, use your profound spiritual
    powers to move more gracefully and easily into your
    next segment of existence. All is well.

Creating Your Life as You Want It To Be

Start right now imagining your life exactly as you want it

to be. The challenge of the time in which we live is no longer

how much pain can we endure, but how big can we dream, how

much joy can we hold, and how long will we let it be that way?

Pain and struggle are familiar to all of us, yet it is not our natu-

ral state. Our natural state is to feel good and to know happiness.

I used to walk around the house repeating between fifty to one

hundred times a day, "I am happy, life is easy, and it is familiar."

I would notice and catch myself making life harder than it had to be and say to myself, *Some part of me is still believing I am a victim and that life has to be hard.* Then I would ask myself, *What do I want?* I want to feel good, I want to be happy, and I want others to feel good just being around me. Then I would translate that into self-affirmations and say to myself, *I am feeling good. I am happy. I am experiencing others feeling good just from being in my presence.*

Whatever you are currently dealing with, know that it no longer has to be hard or take a long time to change. Your intention to feel good right now will be honored, and your life will start to change. Keep coming back to that and think good thoughts as many times as you need to. It will become your reality.

Energy Circles

A powerful process that can change our lives using "I am" statements is called an energy circle. An energy circle is created by drawing an imaginary circle on the ground. Standing outside this imaginary circle, start speaking "I am" statements into the circle to create a hologram of energy. Let's say you want more abundance of health, happiness, positive relationships, money, and time. Draw the circle and, standing outside the circle, speak these statements out loud and throw them into the circle using your hands.

❖ I am grateful for my healthy body.

❖ I am experiencing my body as balanced and free of all disease.

❖ I am experiencing lots of energy and vitality.

❖ I am sleeping easily and I awake feeling refreshed and ready for a new day.

- ❖ I am thin and fit.
- ❖ I am grateful for the feelings of peace and well-being that abound in me.
- ❖ I am seeing the good in all of the events and details of my life.
- ❖ I am a positive person who enjoys the adventure of this life.
- ❖ I am creating more and more experiences that generate feelings of joy.
- ❖ I am attracting like-minded people with whom I love to interact.
- ❖ I am attracting people who are safe and respectful.
- ❖ I share myself easily and I am understood.
- ❖ I am experiencing my intimate relationships as blossoming and growing effortlessly.
- ❖ I am free of all debt.
- ❖ I am creating larger sums of money; money flows easily into my life.
- ❖ I am always flowing in more money than I am flowing out.
- ❖ I am comfortable with money, I spend it in integrity and have fun with it.
- ❖ I am generous in sharing my wealth because I always know there is plenty for me.
- ❖ I am experiencing that I have all the time I need.
- ❖ I move between the different activities of my day easily.
- ❖ I am always on time for my commitments.
- ❖ I am experiencing others as always on time for me.
- ❖ I flow easily within the structure of time in my day.

- ❖ I am grateful to be alive.
- ❖ I am creating more and more of what I want effort-lessly.
- ❖ I am assisted by the powers and spirits of heaven. I ask for their help in all areas of my life. As I ask for what I want, they take care of orchestrating all the details and bring me what I have asked for. I am grateful for this powerful assistance.

After repeating these statements, step into the imaginary circle and the hologram of energy you have just created. Dress yourself in this energy by massaging it into your body from your toes up to your head. Open your arms, embrace this energy, and then close your arms over your heart. Then blow this energy out from your hands, as if you are casting the seeds of it into the ethers of the Universe to start forming and manifesting into your life. As you practice this process daily, you will begin to see evidence of your affirmations develop in your life. As you are in the moment, notice that you are experiencing what you have asked for through your affirmations and complete the cycle of creation by offering out loud or in your heart a prayer of gratitude:

Thank you, God, for assisting me in my creation. I appreciate all the spirits who are helping me experience the full measure of my creative powers.

Start Your Day Positively

Complement your affirmations by starting your day positively. When you wake up, imagine your spiritual crew of angelic support is present in your room, waiting to meet with you. Ask them to assist you with the following:

❖ Bring me ideas of what I want.

❖ Help me connect with like-minded people.

❖ Help me be aware of my power.

❖ Help me be aware of my importance.

❖ Guide me to thoughts that are in harmony with my core desires.

❖ Bring me evidence of how this creation process works in fun, delightful and comfortable ways.

By asking for this help, you will receive it. The Heavens want to assist us in creating that which brings us more joy. They want us to be in a state of joy so we can move through our lives giving joy to more people. Do not sit and wait for God to make your life better. The energy on the planet is the energy of partnering with the heavens. Set an intention to partner with God in creating a wonderful life, and you will experience the miracle of how quickly it can happen.

Creating Wealth

The Universe does not know your bank account status; it only reads the signals you are feeding it. So create a vibration of wealth by playing the following game:

Pretend you have an unlimited supply of $100 bills in your wallet. Every time you spend a $100 bill, imagine another one magically replacing it. Throughout your day, think of the many things you could spend that $100 on. Act as if you are spending it over and over and over. Rejoice and have fun with *all the things you could buy, all the people you could share it with, and all the experiences you could create. As you do this you will send out a vibration of wealth and prosperity that will assist you in creating more wealth.*

You Can Change the Scripts

Many clients say to me, "I can't imagine that person being nice to me, they have always been that way." I will say to them, "What part of you is still believing you deserve to be treated poorly? The only reason it is showing up in your life is because at some level you are believing that is how you deserve to be treated and you keep attracting it!"

I take them through the following visualization process to assist this change:

Imagine your life as a play. You are standing on a stage with all the people in your life standing on the stage with you. Thank everyone for showing up and helping you learn your life lessons. Express gratitude for everyone playing out his or her parts so well. You can even go around the stage and thank each person individually for the lesson they have helped you learn.

Once you have expressed your gratitude, invite all those who have played a part with a negative script to come forward. All those with a negative script are asked to throw these demeaning scripts into a big bonfire. If they are unwilling, they are escorted off the stage by stagehands to create their negative script with someone else.

After the old scripts are gone, Christ is there to hand out new scripts to everyone, including a new script for you. All the new scripts direct everyone to love and honor you and your new script is to receive this love and honor because you now love and honor yourself. Imagine everyone reading through their scripts, getting familiar with the details. Point out to anyone individual details that you would like them to notice so that you can make sure they are aware of the changes in their behavior towards you. Thank everyone for his or her willingness to play off a new script. They all are happy to because they know this is your play and they want to show up how you have asked them to. Have everyone start acting out his or her new parts with you and notice in detail the new healthy behavior you are experiencing in your play. Know at any time that you can stop your play and change the scripts as many times as you want. Always see the people in your play as agreeable and willing to take a new script. If they are not willing to take the new script, have them escorted off your stage.

Create the Life You Really Want

Take the power of your mind, the power of your thoughts, and start creating the life you really want. Catch yourself thinking the worst and ask yourself in that moment, *If I could have anything I want in this situation, what would that look like?* If your will is aligned with God's will and you really believe you deserve it, and believe it can happen, it will. If you doubt it, question it, or keep your attention on what has still not happened for you, it will kink up the energy and you will not receive it. Become the deliberate creator of your life. Anticipate your future, one second ahead or one year ahead, and be as specific and deliberate as it is possible to be and still feel good. Take time every day to identify your dominant intentions free of worrying about how they're going to show up. When you ask the powers of heaven to work on your behalf and to take care of the details, they will produce for you what you have asked for.

Preventing Conflict in Your Marriage

You have co-created the current state of your marriage. The next time you are starting to get at each other, stop yourself. Say to your spouse, "I love you and respect you. I don't want to do this anymore. I want to create a loving and honoring relationship with you. What do you want?" If your spouse is cold to you, they have inner-child states existing subconsciously within them that are wounded. Any time you are in a conflict in a marriage, you both are in the energy of a wounded inner-child. All you can do at this point is protect yourself from getting hurt again.

Ideas to Improve Your Marriage

To support your marriage thriving, try doing all or some of the following:

1. Pray together as a couple out loud, each taking turns, at least once a day.
2. Praise your spouse with all the wonderful things you wish they would say to you.
3. Create a new script for them by writing in detail what

you believe your ideal companion would be like. Live by that script yourself.

4. Ask each other what one thing you say or do that hurts them deeply. Choose never to say or do it again.

5. Create "What We Want More of" lists. Ask the Heavens to help you create them.

6. Stop talking about what's not working or what you don't want. Start talking about what's working and what you want more of.

7. Choose to say only positive things to others about your spouse.

8. If you find you create conflict at the same time or place in your home, start clearing the patterns by noticing it and stopping it. For example, if you always fight about money in the evening in the bedroom, agree not to recreate that again. Talk about money Saturday morning as you go for a walk together. Set an intention. It will be a harmonious, successful experience.

9. Have sex a lot because you enjoy it.

10. Play together often. Go on a date night alone once a week.

11. Take a trip for just the two of you once a year.

Ideas to Improve Your Family Life

The following are a few ideas to help strengthen your family:

1. Pray together as a family once each day. In our family of

six people, we each take a day of the week to say all the prayers for that day: family prayer, prayer at meals, and any other prayers. "Whose day is it to pray?" is heard often at our house.

2. Eat together at a sit-down meal at least three times a week. More often is even better.

3. Tell each of your children individually, "If there is anything I say or do that makes you feel worthless or not good enough, stop me and tell me. I love you and want to treat you with respect and honor."

4. Have a family activity once a week: anything—cleaning up the yard, going to the movies, reading a book together, watching old family videos, or doing something for someone else.

5. Let your children witness often how much you love and respect their mom or dad.

6. When one of your children comes to you dissatisfied with their current life experience, rather than sympathizing with them and talking about what they don't want, which will only help them create more of it, say to them, "Why are you creating this? If you could have it the way you want it, what would that look like?" Help them become aware that they, with God, are the creators of their lives.

7. Take car trips together where everybody is together a lot!

8. Most of the time when you vacation, go only with your family so that your children are focused on each other and their friendships can grow.

9. Never use demeaning or derogatory language or voice tones with each other. Hostile humor is saying something negative in a funny way. It is really shame with laughter. If someone is using a negative voice tone, politely say, "Please change your tone."

10. Hug your children every day. Better yet, tuck them in bed, no matter what age they are.

Gratitude Processes

1. Appreciate everything.

2. Express gratitude for every single moment of your life. The more you create feelings of appreciation and gratitude, the more you will attract into your life that which you can appreciate and for which you can feel gratitude.

3. Gratitude is one of the highest vibrations in which we can be. Look for things for which you can be grateful. As you're driving along, play the Grateful Game. By yourself or with others, take turns saying what you are grateful for.

4. Start a Gratitude Journal. Every Thanksgiving, as a family, we get out our Gratitude Journal and write 1,000 things for which we are grateful. We number from one to 1,000, leave it on the kitchen counter with a pen, and family members and friends are invited to write in it as often as they would like. It usually takes us between a week and ten days to get to 1,000.

5. In your prayers, thank God for believing in you, for giving you the agency to create your life, and for remembering your truth.

6. Thank all the people who have shown up in your life to play their parts for you.

7. Write a thank-you note once a week to someone to express your appreciation for them.

8. Appreciate yourself for what you are remembering and for the joys you are creating

Having Conversations with God

1. Pray to God in the name of Jesus Christ. Start your prayer by calling upon the father by saying, "Dear God," "Dear Heavenly Father," or "Father in Heaven." Close your prayers in the name of Jesus Christ by saying, "I offer this prayer In the name of Jesus Christ, amen."

2. Try thanking God for what you want in a manner that shows you believe it is coming. A prayer of pure gratitude would make every expression one of thanks. As you pray from a place of pure gratitude, you believe that what you want will be given. As you thank God ahead of time, you are trusting that he loves you and wants to bless your life with that which is desirable to you.

3. In a meditation or visualization, you can be with God to receive guidance and direction from him. Visualize yourself standing in a place of light in the Heavens. Imagine God standing before you. Since he is your father, he would want to give you a hug. Let him hug you. Imagine God holding you as long as it feels good. Imagine God listening to you as you share what you want to talk to him about. Imagine him responding, counseling, and giving loving feedback.

4. A conversation is communication with at least two indi-
    viduals. If you desire to have conversations with God, you
    will have to pay attention to how he is going to talk back
    to you. Expect God to reply. Too often people experience
    prayer as a one-way solicitation to the heavens without
    expecting a definite response.

5. Take time each day to be still, and quiet your mind for
    ten to fifteen minutes. This practice will open and make
    clearer the channel you have to heaven. As this channel
    to heaven becomes stronger and clearer you will hear the
    voice of God in your mind and in your heart. He will
    manifest the truth of all things to you all through your day.

6. Keep a conversations-with-God journal. Write your
    questions in it and God's responses. The response may
    not come immediately, but it will come. Write your
    question and know that you will soon be given the answer.
    Know that your answer from God will manifest
    effortlessly and sometimes when least expected in a
    number of creative ways. As you look back through your
    journal, you will notice that what you used to be unclear
    about is now very clear to you.

7. Talk to God all through your day silently in your mind.
    This silent exchange will sustain you in making choices
    and behaving in a manner that is harmonious with your
    core desires.

A Process to Clear Your Generational Depression

Imagine yourself standing in the light with a higher power
(Jesus Christ, angels, God, or Holy Spirit). Ask your generations

that have lived before you to come into the light. Imagine all these people in the light with you. Ask your higher self of all the depression you have experienced, how much of it is generational and how much is your own. You will get two numbers that equal 100 percent. For most people the generational percent is more than 50 percent and their part is less than 50 percent. It is usually 70/30 or 80/20. Tell your ancestors you are choosing to clear this pattern from the family.

Draw a picture of a garbage can on a sketchpad. Place the pattern of depression—with all the negative beliefs and emotions that you have experienced with it—into the garbage can. When this is all in the garbage can, enlarge the picture of the garbage can as big as you can imagine it. Look at it as an observer and say, "It's just energy. I am not in the picture. I am the one looking at the picture." Now create a blowtorch in your mind, set your picture on fire, and watch it burn into ashes. Take the ashes and spread them on the ground. Watch beautiful flowers grow up through the ashes returning life-giving energy to you and your ancestors. Imagine every cell in your body being filled with life-giving energy. How does that feel? Imagine your ancestors cheering for you and congratulating you on your choosing to clear this pattern.

The Five-Step Process To Create More
of What You Want in Life

1. Find your desire and know what you want. If you don't know, ask to know! Tune-in and feel if what you are wanting is timely and appropriate for the highest and greatest good of your life.

2. Ask for it—ask God, ask your angels, ask the Universe.

3. Believe it will show up without having to know when and how. If you have doubt or fear or "have" to have it, let go of the have-to and energize your belief so it can and will show up.

4. Trust and allow it—get out of the way and let synchronicity start to play out. Only "do" something to help it happen when you feel prompted to.

5. Receive it in gratitude—when it does show up say thank you to God, angels, and the Universe.

Appendix of Helpful Resources

I have found the following resources to be very beneficial to my family and myself.

Rapid Eye Technology
Rapid Eye Institute
3748 74th Ave. S.E.
Salem, OR 97301
888-399-1181
email: RETCampus@aol.com
www.rapideye.org
International Registry to find a
practitioner near you:
www.rapideye.org

Aromatherapy Essential Oils
Young Living Essential Oils
250 S. Main St.
Payson, UT 84651
800-763-9963
www.youngliving.com
To purchase products as a
consumer or distributor, use
referral #12571

Super Blue Green Algae
Cell Tech
1300 Main Street
Klamath Falls, OR 97601
800-800-1300
www.celltech.com
To purchase products as a
consumer or distributor, use
referral # 304647

Therapeutic Gemstones
Gemisphere
2812 NW Thurman St.
Portland, OR 97209
800-727-8877
www.gemisphere.com

Energy Medicine
Innersource
P.O. Box 213
Ashland, OR 97520
800-835-8332
www.innersource.net

ABOUT THE AUTHOR

Carol is a motivating speaker to both youth and adults. She feels that one of her greatest gifts is a teacher. She has many times commented at the end of one her speaking engagements, "Boy, I learned a lot from myself tonight!" She believes our greatest truths are awakened and taught to ourselves. She admonishes her audiences to trust that all truth resides within us. Anything we hear someone else share that rings true for us, is only true because we already hold the truth within us.

Carol Tuttle is a Certified Master level Rapid Eye Technician and practitioner of energy psychology and energy medicine. She has had a successful private practice for many years. She currently works with clients on a limited basis.

As a teacher, author, and spiritual therapist she has assisted thousands of people in creating the lives they want and deserve. Carol, a graduate of Brigham Young University has taught high school, owned small businesses, and has been a counseling specialist at the Utah State Prison. She is an avid tennis player, marathon runner, and fitness buff. Carol lives in Sandy, Utah with her fabulous husband Jon and their wonderful and incredible four children.

Contact information for Carol Tuttle:

Carol Tuttle
P.O. Box 900546
Sandy, UT 84090-0128
email: carol@caroltuttle.com
Web site: www.caroltuttle.com

To attend a **Remembering Wholeness** seminar or,
to learn more about hosting a seminar in your area go to:
www.caroltuttle.com

To inquire about Carol's availability for speaking engagements,
email: carol@caroltuttle.com

For information on private sessions with Carol, email:
carol@caroltuttle.com

Please send Carol your healing stories, your angel stories,
and your miracle stories, which either resulted from reading this
book, attending one of Carol's seminars, or having Rapid Eye
sessions. Send them to the above address or email them to:
carol@caroltuttle.com

This book, *Remembering Wholeness* and many of Carol's
Remembering Wholeness seminars are available on audio. For
more information, go to: www.caroltuttle.com